The Ultimate Weight Loss Solution

Are You Ready?

Dan Aguilera

Dedication

I've dedicated this book to my Family and Friends who have supported me through both my personal and professional growth and my beautiful daughter Maria who lights up my life.

Thank you also to my past and present clients who have contributed to my ongoing education and experience, all of which I am truly grateful.

Contents

Acknowledgments

I remember when I was first introduced to the fitness industry over 15 years ago. I was overwhelmed with the mass of conflicting advice and I looked at the leaders, hoping that I one day would have their knowledge and skill. But, one thing I have since learned is that the industry, both then and now, is still preaching very much the same thing – nothing original or cutting edge as they would like you to believe.

Cutting Out the Rubbish (That's Me)

Something that I find really interesting is that in society now it is normal for us to be overweight and unhealthy. When did this become normal?

I'm not about re-packaging old content, I'm about building functional fitness strategies that work for the masses and do not require expensive equipment or specialist nutritional ingredients; I'm about using what you already have access to and what's within reach for most.

I know that if you have to add more to your already busy life, then it's unlikely that you'll able to commit, not because you don't want to but because you just can't. Most people live their life in a state of overwhelm. There is too much information out there particularly when it comes to weight loss, so much contradicting information, you only have to type 'weight loss' into Google and you will get 269,000,000 results in (0.72 seconds). That's a lot of information and most of the information is either funded by the sugar companies or a supplement company of some kind, promoting magic shakes or pills.

It's because of this that I acknowledge not the working professionals within the fitness industry or the highly qualified and skilled nutritionists, but every person who spends the time and commits to making a programme work for them. That's you.

It's you that I'm grateful for; the feedback you provide inspires me to reach out and help all those willing to listen. I acknowledge those who listen, commit and perform – thank you and good luck.

Introduction

When I started out in my career I didn't know how much of an impact I would have on those I worked with, I was just excited about what I was able to offer through my passion for learning and my motivation to improve the life of those around me.

I'm a realist and despite being aware of the many different quick fix solutions out there, this is not an approach you will encounter with me. If you've signed up to my programme then you're in it for the long-haul. Back in the day I used to sell meal replacement shakes, this was before I became obsessed with Nutrition and Health. I now have a code of practice I set in place for myself and refuse to change despite continual on-going pressure to sell the 'quick fix' solution that seem to be sold by people who do not even work within the health and fitness industry – not naming any well-known weight loss shakes.

I've been very fortunate along my path to work with some amazing people, including my current and past clients, friends and family whom I've often bored with my constant excitement about the topic and my inner desire to improve the lives of those around me, yet they ultimately benefited – whether they liked it or not.

I'm serious about nutrition, fitness and lifestyle performance…

During sessions with one of my initial clients, it dawned on me that there was a serious issue with 'health and fitness' education here in the UK. Nutritional advice was hard to come by and I came to the realisation that the masses of conflicting fitness advice created a minefield for anyone genuinely trying to find a simple solution.

It was because of this that my goal shifted from just providing set exercises to looking at the whole picture. I gave up working with those with one goal – to lose weight quickly – and focused on working with those who wanted to improve their life for the better and for the long-term.

"Fat doesn't live on a healthy body, so let's focus on becoming really healthy"

Taking this approach separated me from the majority of 'fit-pros' and I'm glad. I'm glad because my clients have one of the highest success rates in the country and benefit from not only getting fit but meeting a new path of life that offers an abundance of lifestyle changes.

Once you have been a coach for a decent length of time you've seen all the diets and training protocols come full circle, you come to realise that there's only ONE program of diet and nutrition that TRULY works for people...

The one they STICK to!

It's expected that nearly 80% of the UK will be obese within the next 15 years. Why? Well, I'll cover all of the aspects within this book, hopefully removing you from this statistic in the process.

When were you taught to be healthy?

....

What type of lifestyle are you sold on a daily basis?

....

Nothing in life is guaranteed but what you do today controls your life in the future and therefore influences what you are likely to become. You have the choice right now whether to improve or not. The action you take today directly influences your life tomorrow – it really is as simple as that.

Taking the right action today will change the way you live your life moving forward; you can either carry on living your life the way you are now and staying as you are now or you can take action today to change. Ultimately, the choice is yours to make.

We humans are the problem – we accept what is being sold to us without questioning it.

I believe this book will change the way you think about your life and your ability to achieve, and it will hopefully inspire you to move forward with a healthier and more fulfilling life.

Best wishes

Dan

Chapter One

It has been just under 2 years since Dan gave me the confidence and support to step on the scales for the first time aged 28, since then with his guidance and knowledge I have gone from 23 stone to being in the 13 stone bracket. I continue to learn from him and understand more about my health, fitness and approach to detoxing and nutrition than I could have imagined. He has helped make me a better person and given me the energy to fully enjoy my time with my beautiful family. I can't speak highly enough of the positive impact Dan has had in my life, Thank you Dan. Sam C

How This Book Works For You

Within this book I will be questioning some of the things you may believe to be true and for this reason there may be some points that contradict much of what you've read, heard, learnt or even think about what you know about health and weight loss.
However, I ask that you trust me.

We are going to cut through all the fluff, give you just enough education to empower you to make DRAMATIC changes, and set you on a path that will allow you to adjust it to your life and make individual adjustments along the way.

We'll be looking at functional fitness. This is a term I use a lot and it represents something that's really important to me and the message I deliver. For example, if you are currently 23 stone, then I'm not going to ask you to train for a marathon in 12 weeks, likewise, if you are underweight and want to gain muscle, I'm not going to recommend fasting. Functional fitness is all about providing each individual with the information needed to achieve their individual goals through a combination of education, accountability and practical advice that will work within their life. We're all different and it would be unfair of me to ask everyone to follow the same programme. Only *you* can decide what *you* want to achieve.

I will be covering simple science but this isn't anything you should be worried about as I'll be sticking to the basics and going into just enough depth to keep you interested. We'll go through a lot of information quickly with the emphasis being on grasping the relevance of what is being said rather than delving into deeper scientific issues. Of course, you can always choose to do further research on areas that particularly interest you.

Here are some questions to help kick-start your thinking:

If you know that it's bad to eat processed foods that are high in Sugar, why do you do it?

....

....

What is your motivation to lose weight and improve your health?

....

....

....

What It Takes To Achieve True Transformation

Transforming your body is more than just a workout and diet plan. If you want to achieve a true transformation, you need to have drive, commitment, motivation, and intensity.

There are 4 key factors that play into your transformation.

1. Progressive Nutrition
2. Progressive Exercise
3. Education and Support
4. Lifestyle and Behaviour Change

It is my goal to be able to help you modify all four of these factors to ensure that you are setting yourself up for success.

The Price Of Success

Change is a door that can only be opened from the inside - Terry Neil

People say to me all of the time that they want to lose weight and transform their bodies.
The first challenge they face is their current readiness to change. Are you prepared to go through what you need to do to achieve your goal? Are you willing to pay the price?

It is important that you understand this concept of paying the price. Where you are today and what you have in your life is a result of all the choices and decisions you have made;

"Your body is a direct reflection of what you put into it daily, so the nutrition, exercise and lifestyle choices you are making today are causing you to have the body you currently have." - Dan Aguilera

It is where you have wanted to be, if only subconsciously. Therefore if you are going to change, you need to accept that you are going to have to leave behind some things that you like! Or think you need. This means that you are going to have to put some significant effort in to achieving what you want.

Excuses

Let's be honest from the very beginning – you're busy. I know this. I also know you've tried lots of diets before – and you've been told they're the best! You want results but deep down you know that committing to something that doesn't interest you isn't going to work – despite knowing it's something you *should* be doing. This is a common issue, and it's one of the reasons you have perhaps yo-yo dieted in the past.

> *"Excuses are the lies we tell ourselves, to make ourselves feel better about something we have or haven't done"*

I'm not going to patronise you with endless facts about the scientific structure of the molecule, nor am I going to tell you that you need to achieve a six-pack in order to be normal. What I will do is provide you with workable strategies that have helped my clients achieve the lasting results they want. There isn't a set programme for you to follow but instead, a set of strategies designed to help you get from where you are now to where you want to be.

Why are you unhappy with the weight you are?

....

....

What have you done to really change in the past?

....

....

Why do your diets usually fail?

....

....

....

I want you to stop right now: stop reading: stop what you're thinking about, and just read over the answers you've given above. Immerse yourself in each question and really think about the reasons *why*...Now answer the following:

Why is now the right time to change?

....

Why can't I allow this to continue anymore?

....

What do I need to do to ensure I change for good?

....

....

"Definiteness of purpose is the starting point of all achievement."
–W. Clement Stone

Chapter Two

"Since joining the gym with Dan it's changed my whole outlook on eating and exercise. I love the training sessions and always feel I'm pushed to get the best out of me. Never before have I enjoyed exercise like Dan's sessions... He is so motivating and supportive but also truthful... He doesn't talk rubbish and that's exactly what I need!!! A couple months in and I'm already getting results. I'm currently on the cleanse and loving it and then will be hitting the 6wk challenge... All thanks to Dan" Siobhan W.

Progressive Nutrition

Nutrition counts for 60-80% of the way you look and feel, so it's the key to you achieving the results you desire.

Very often I see people go on extreme diets where they cut out all of the foods they enjoy, then something comes up and breaks their pattern such as a Birthday, Holiday or Party and they completely fall off the wagon and can't get back on.

Sound familiar?

The word progressive is the key thing here; you are not expected to cut out everything you like. It is more effective to look at your nutrition plan organically and create a long-term healthy lifestyle change, which includes structured treats.

Follow my 80/20 Rule

80% of the time follow the healthy nutrition principles and allow 20% for structured treats, 20% will never outweigh 80% unless you just go on a binge and eat everything in sight.

Why Are We Overweight

There are 2 main hormones in the body that control whether you gain weight or lose weight. The first one is Insulin, which a lot of people have heard of through diabetes, and the second one is called Glucagon.

Now before I go into those what I want to do is talk through what most people typically eat on a daily basis. Most of the people I see will predominantly have cereal for breakfast, some form of crisps or chocolate for a snacks, a sandwich for their lunch and for dinner some form of pasta dish, that's typical of about 95% of people who first come to see me to lose weight.

When we are looking at foods we need to break them down into 3 food groups essentially.

The first one is **Carbohydrates.**

Carbohydrates are anything that grow from the ground, so any wheat based products, things like your bread, pasta, rice, cereal, potatoes, you have also got more fibrous carbohydrates like fruit, vegetables and salad then you also have things like biscuits, crisps, chocolates, sweets, cakes, fizzy drinks and ice cream.

So they all sit in the carbohydrate box

The second one is **Proteins**

Proteins are anything with eyes and a mouth and come from a meat source things like chicken, fish, turkey, eggs, beef, lamb, pork. Then you have also got some plant based proteins such as chickpeas, lentils and tofu.

So they all sit in the protein box

Then we have **Fats.**

Fats are things like nuts and seeds, avocado, olive oil, butters, dressings and spreads.

And they sit in the fat box

So if we were to break down most people's typical days, here is what we would find

B- a bowl of cereal, we know that's pretty much 100% carbohydrates
S- a bar of chocolate again that's 100% carbohydrates
L- Tuna or chicken sandwich, would be around 80% carbohydrates
S – a bag of crisps again 100% carbohydrates
D – Pasta or spaghetti bolognaise again mainly carbohydrates so about 80%

Most of the people I see typically have 80% carbohydrates on a daily basis, now let me explain to you what carbohydrates are and their role in the body:

Carbohydrates no matter what you eat, whether you eat biscuits, crisps, chocolate, cake, pasta, bread, potatoes or cereal are all the same thing, your body cant tell the difference between any of those foods and at the end of the day they all end up as sugar in the body.

Let's explore how this all works...

When you eat your first meal of the day, (which are predominantly carbohydrates), that comes into the body and your body breaks that down to sugar. From there that raises your blood sugar levels up high, at the high point your body says that there is too much sugar in the blood and I need to get rid of that so it produces the hormone Insulin. Insulin's role is to the lower blood sugar levels, so insulin says to the body there is too much sugar in the blood and I need to get rid of this sugar.

Insulin then stores this sugar into three pots, the first pot it fills up is in the liver. Now the function of your liver is for the brain and the vital organs so the most important thing to the body is, get enough sugar in the liver to feed the brain throughout the day The second pot is for the muscle cell, we know we need sugar in the muscles to enable us to be able to move on a daily basis otherwise we wouldn't be able to do anything.

The real trouble with these two pots is that they only have a limited capacity to store sugar, which means they can only store a little bit.

All of the excess sugar then goes into the third pot which is the FAT pot, we know that pot has an unlimited capacity to store sugar which is why we are now seeing people weighing 20, 30, 40 or 50 stone.

You are continuously getting excess dietary sugars stored as fat within the body.

Now whenever insulin is produced it always produces too much and it drops your blood sugar levels down low, at this low point your body goes into something called hypoglycaemia (which is low blood sugar levels) typical symptoms of hypoglycaemia are lack of concentration, mood swings, tiredness, headaches, craving sugary types of foods, sound familiar?

Most of the people I see experience these symptoms around 3-4 times a day on some level as I'm sure most of you do as well. What you then do is have your next meal, which again are predominantly carbohydrates, which lift you back up, then you will go back down, back up, back down, back up, back down.

So what you are doing throughout your day is what we call sugar spiking and every time insulin is produced at the top, all the excess dietary sugar is converted as FAT.

Now our body is really clever, it doesn't just store fat for no reason, it doesn't just say let's have fun with everyone and make everyone store fat, it stores fat for this reason, for every 1g of fat is worth 9 calories of energy, 1g of carbohydrates is 4 calories of energy and 1g of protein is also 4 calories, so your body will naturally want to use fat as its main energy source.

The trouble we all face is that we eat the same things day after day therefore gaining weight over a period of time, you don't just wake up one day and all of a sudden you are carrying 2, 3, 5 or 10 stone, it comes on you bit by bit until one day you look in the mirror and say actually I need to make certain changes, which is why you are reading this book.

So the key thing what we must understand is what makes us overweight! We now know it's not fat that makes us FAT, it's carbohydrates that are broken down into sugar which makes us overweight.

> *"Low Fat diets are Get Fat diets, because they replace the fat with Carbohydrates which are essentially just sugar"*

So we really now need to begin to understand how much sugar we are eating on a daily basis, we do this by a rule called the divide by 5 rule.

If you divide the total grams of carbohydrates minus the fibre by 5, it equals the teaspoons of sugar in something. Let's put this in perspective; the average person in the UK consumes 500-600g of Carbohydrates per day, which is 100-120 teaspoons of sugar per day.

For effective fat loss your body only really needs 20-30 teaspoons of sugar per day, so as a nation we are overeating around 100 teaspoons of sugar per day, which is why we are getting bigger and bigger.

The Solution to Weight Loss Through Nutrition

> *"The doctors of the future will give no medicine but interest their patients in the care of the human frame, in diet and in the cause and prevention of disease"* -
> Thomas Edison

This is where the second hormone Glucagon is important.

What we must start to do is balance our meals out, and the correct ration for Fat loss is 40% Carbohydrates, 30% Protein and 30% Fat.

Now at the moment you are probably looking at that and thinking, how do I actually make a meal out of that?

First of all I'm going to talk to you about the science behind this, then I'm going to talk about how you are going make those meals in the real world, in the world where it fits in with your lifestyle, because at the end of the day I can sit here and Wow you with science but if you can't make those meals relative in the real world it doesn't mean anything it's just science.

So let's talk about the science part first -

If you eat a meal at 40/30/30 what happens is you balance your blood sugar levels, so you won't be getting the highs and you certainty won't be getting any lows that you are currently feeling either. Now a lot of the time people think this is only about weight loss but actually it's also about how you feel and if you keep getting highs and lows you know that effects the quality of your life because it effects your energy levels, it effects how you feel, it gives you headaches and things like that.

So not only are we going to stop that by stabilising your blood sugar levels we are going to teach you how we are going to burn fat as energy which is the real key thing.

Now as your blood sugar levels start to drop the body is really clever, the body actually says that there is not enough sugar in blood and it needs to do something about it, so it produces the opposite hormone to insulin called glucagon.

Glucagon says to the body that there isn't enough sugar in the blood and can't allow the blood sugar levels to drop down to low, so glucagon goes into your fat stores and turns the fat back into sugar, so you actually start to burn fat as energy.

Here is the real clever part, per meal you eat at 40/30/30 you burn 70 calories of fat, now let me put that in perspective for you. To burn 70 calories of fat running on a treadmill, you would need to run for about an hour because 70 fat calories is the equivalent to about 780 calories on a cardio piece of equipment. It will take most people about an hour to do that.

So if you can eat 5 meals per day at 40/30/30 you will burn 350 calories of Fat per day for FREE and the reason its for free is because this is all based on nutritional science alone, it's got nothing to do with exercise. It's to do with balancing the master hormones within the body that control whether you gain weight or lose weight. So it is hormonal fat loss, which is the key thing here and is the most effective way of burning fat.

So that's the science taken care off, now let's talk about 40/30/30 in the real world.

The simplest was to explain 40/30/30 is if you take the palm of your hand and that is the protein, then take one clenched fist of vegetables, a cupped handful of carbohydrates and your thumb of fat in terms of your portion sizes.

Serving Sizes

So, what is a serving?

A serving size equals the following:

> 1 serving of protein = the palm of your hand
> 1 serving of carbohydrates = a cupped handful
> 1 serving of vegetables = 1 clenched fist
> 1 serving of fat = 1 thumb

Recommended Food Sources

Proteins

Lean Minced Beef (90% or leaner), Cuts of beef, Chicken, Turkey, Tuna Steaks, Eggs* (1 to 2 lge = 1 serving), Sardines, Prawns, Salmon *, Pork, Beef Jerky, Lamb *, Quorn products, Tempah or Tofu, Natural Yoghurt *, Tinned Tuna, Crab, Quinoa, Edamame Beans, Soba Noodles. *includes 1 serving of fat as well.

Carbohydrates

Most Fruits, Wholegrain Rice, Sweet Potatoes, Oatmeal , Quinoa Tortilla (1 med = 1 serving), Beans, Pumpkin, Sweet Corn, Butternut Squash, Spaghetti, Vegetables, Spinach, Broccoli,, Cauliflower, Peppers, Onion, Tomato, Cucumbers, Courgette, Yellow Squash, Asparagus, Brussel Sprouts, Green Beans, Peas, Carrots, Artichoke, Aubergine, Celery, Kale, Romaine, Cabbage, Pak Choi, Watercress, Radishes, Turnip, Parsley, Shallots, Sauerkraut, Mushrooms, Salsa

Fats

Extra Virgin Olive Oil, Coconut Oil, Nut Butters (almond, cashew, peanut), Raw mixed nuts, Avocado, Butter (grass fed if possible), Cheeses, Pumpkin Seeds, Sunflower seeds, Chia Seeds

Substitutes

Substitute cows milk with unsweetened almond or almond coconut blend milk.

This is what I have found to be a great starting point for most of our clients. This allows you to get in an adequate amount of food and makes your transition easier. If you are just starting out on your weight loss plan or new to our program this is where you should start.

Women

3-4 servings of lean protein
2-3 servings of carbohydrates
4-6 servings of vegetables
2-3 servings of fat

Men

4-6 servings of lean protein
2-3 servings of carbohydrates
6-8 servings of vegetables
4-6 servings of fat

The Science Of Food

Why Do We Eat?

> *"Let food be your medicine and medicine be your food"*
> Hippocrates

In the most simplistic terms we eat because we need to – at a deeper level, and in a more natural sense, our craving is survival (taste is a craving that has evolved over time). The primary role and purpose of food is the production of energy. The foods we eat are processed by our digestive system to extract the energy which is then distributed to the rest of our body to enable us to function. Obviously, it's a little more complicated than that but we don't need to go into the intricacies of biochemistry for the purposes of this book. However, it's a really interesting subject and I would recommend taking the time to read more about it when you advance.

The digestion process can be broken down into five broad stages:

1. We consume food via the mouth. This is chewed and swallowed to begin its journey through to the stomach and so on.
2. Glucose is extracted from the consumed food (highlighting the importance of consuming quality food).
3. Glucose is passed around the body via the bloodstream by

demand.

4. Energy is extracted and used.

5. Any unused energy is stored as fat (highlighting the importance of regulating the amount consumed).

In brief, you can see how over indulgence, lack of movement and fat retention are linked. This is something we'll explore in more detail later. For now, the important message to take on board is that the amount you consume, the amount used, and the amount stored all start out as the choice you make to introduce the food into your system.

Notice the language here, 'you', 'your'…

Throughout the book you will notice the language I use indicates that *you* have to take ownership over your diet. Reading the book is a great start but it's the actions you take as a result of reading it that will create the impact you desire.

What Is Digestion?

Digestion can be described simply as the process of breaking food down to a point at which the body can absorb the nutrients contained within it. The sight and smell of food sets off the digestive enzymes in your mouth and along with chewing natural, whole foods this instigates the breakdown of substrates into absorbable molecules.

Saliva also plays an important role at this stage as it contains enzymes which work to further break down the fats and carbohydrates.

When the food becomes broken down enough to be swallowed, it passes through the throat into the stomach. This is where the real magic happens: the food is further broken down by a number of liquids produced by the stomach, each one with its own role to play. The makeup of the food determines the speed at which it will be broken down but as a basic guide, carbohydrates are processed faster than protein and protein faster than fat.

As the food leaves the stomach, it's pretty much in a refined liquid form. It passes into the gastrointestinal tract where most of the absorption happens. There are many different levels of absorption but for the moment we're going to focus only on the absorption of glucose.

Glucose is absorbed through the cell walls and used to make energy. In the same way that you refuel your car according to the distance you've travelled and the distance you've yet to travel, your body needs to be refuelled according to its energy needs. If you don't refuel it often enough, you're going to break down, but if you overfill it in one refuelling, it's going to spill over. Of course, this is an overly simplistic breakdown of the whole process but providing in depth information on the role of mitochondria and membranes at this stage would only lead to you feeling overwhelmed and more likely to switch off. I'm choosing to keep it simple because I want you to stay switched on to the idea of following through with the recommendations I make.

Why is it important that I consume the right amount of food for my energy output (distance travelled)?

....

....

Could this be part of the reason why I've gained weight in the past?

....

....

What changes can I make to ensure that when I move more I consume more, and consume less when I move less?

....

....

Insulin Explained

When I mention insulin, most people think about diabetes. Insulin is a complex subject covering a wide variety of factors but, in a nutshell, insulin is needed to enable glucose (sugar) to enter the body's cells to make energy. However, in modern western cultures there is now an issue arising over having too much glucose (sugar) in the body as the excess is stored as fat. Insulin can also cause an increase in appetite, and this can of course be a major issue for those looking to control or lose weight – especially if they don't manage the production of insulin consciously.

So why is insulin important? Well, insulin grabs excess glucose (sugar) in the blood and stores it in the liver and as glycogen in the muscles all of the excess glucose is stored as FAT. This naturally leads to a drop in the insulin levels in the blood, which in turn causes a signal to be sent to the brain to trigger an increase in appetite and the need to eat. Consuming a daily diet of sugary fast foods can create an imbalance known as insulin resistance, which is now a major cause of obesity and cardiovascular illnesses in the modern world.

Eating a quality diet free of highly processed and refined foods can massively change the way insulin is produced and used by the body. Insulin can be thought of as a tin miner in the body, breaking down the sugars and passing them on to be used immediately as fuel or storing them away for later use. The more sugar there is for the tin miner to deal with, the more there is to be stored away when it's not needed, and all of this leads to an untidy workplace on a cellular level.

Quality in and quality out; rubbish in and rubbish out.

So what's the solution? When you think about it, removing ALL processed foods and foods that are high in sugar from your diet is the simplest and most straightforward way to help the tin miner get his workplace in order. Replacing those foods with fresh, non-processed foods containing only natural sugars and minerals gives the body the energy supplies it needs without the clutter of excess making the tin miner's job harder than it needs to be.

What foods do I consume that are high in refined (or white) sugars?

....

....

Would now be a good time to remove them from my diet?

....

....

What naturally grown foods (that I like) could I replace them with?

....

....

When can I implement this change in my diet?

....

....

Important note: when removing processed and 'fake' foods from your diet, you're going to experience a number of shifts within the body. Just as a drug addict goes through a withdrawal, you'll experience a similar effect with the impact generally leading to symptoms such as headaches, mood swings and emotional ups and downs. This isn't anything to be concerned about and the symptoms usually ease after only a couple of days. Keep in mind that any negative effects you experience are only temporary and they are simply the by-product of your body craving and detoxing at the same time.

What Is Glycogen?

As glucose levels build up within the blood, insulin takes on a second role. The glucose that can't be absorbed through the cell walls is converted into glycogen which is essentially the short-term fuel source used by the body in everyday activities. Only limited amounts of glycogen are stored by the body as it's in constant use which means that stored sugars (fat) are called upon when fuel supplies are low. The more active we are and the more we deplete glycogen supplies, the more we use stored sugar (glucose) supplies, thus controlling the build-up of fat held within the body. We will cover this in greater detail later in the book.

It's the additional fitness activities we take part in that are usually most relevant here. As we increase the energy requirement of the body, the more likely it is that we'll begin dipping into the body's fat reserves to fuel the additional activity. However, it can take newcomers to exercise a little while to begin reaping the rewards of 'fat burning' in this way as it takes repeated additional energy demands to effectively shock the body into letting go of reserves.

Increasing our activity levels or simply moving more changes the dynamics of energy production and this, along with a change in diet from fake sugars to natural sugars, brings with it MASSIVE results.

Why is fitness important to the fat burning process?

....

What can I do to increase the movement within my normal working day?

....

What adjustments should I make to ensure that my body doesn't store additional sugars?

....

In Summary

The process is as follows:

Food is consumed - glucose is produced - circulates within the blood - enters the cells - used as fuel (energy).

Keeping optimum levels of glucose in your blood is essential in your weight loss journey. The more aware you become and the more knowledgeable you are in terms of how your body functions, the more likely it is that you will be able to consciously control your food choices and ultimately reduce your sugar intake.

It's quite possible that the above information is all stuff you already knew but there's a big difference between *knowing* about something and *doing* something about it, right? The only thing that's important now is that you make a conscious decision to change; you must choose to make changes for the better and you must *commit* to following through on your choice. The more leverage you create in this choice, the less likely you are to relapse into old habits along the way.

What Are Food Groups?

Something I'm regularly asked to explain is the difference between one type of food and another. This is often because people struggle to create a healthy balance in their daily diet and it's something we'll look at in more detail later but for now, try asking yourself the question below. Very often, the answer to this one question is all you need to help you figure out whether you're making a good food choice.

Will this make me fat?

....

....

Now, I appreciate the harshness of this question but the reality is that you need to start looking at your food with a completely different set of eyes – and you need to start asking better questions. For example, if a pizza has rocket and pineapple on it, does that make it a healthy choice; do 'light' versions of cheese or butter make a food the right choice? The answer is no.

We often over complicate food but making good choices needn't be hard. In fact, understanding food choices is the easiest aspect of weight loss but, that being said, there are three food groups you need to be aware of to help you make better choices – carbohydrates, proteins and fats. Each food group acts differently and has a different role within the body, and ultimately each group is broken down at a different speed thus providing the body with the right things at the right times.

In order (based on most foods):

> Carbohydrates are usually the first to be broken down as they provide the 'instant' energy needed for everyday functioning.

> Proteins are usually the second to be broken down and they are used to build and repair all areas of the body.

> Fats are the last to broken down and they are used as insulation and energy reserves.

Now let's look at these in a little more detail, but again it's my intention to keep things simple and relevant. My recommendations are just that, recommendations, and it must always be remembered that the best diet for you is one that will last forever; a diet that will keep you motivated to eat well and make better choices every day.

What Are Carbohydrates?

Carbohydrates are generally divided into two categories and are the main source of glucose. They are made from groups of sugars that are linked in varying lengths and as a result perform differently depending on the lifestyle you lead and environmental factors. Carbohydrates are usually sourced from widely grown crops and offer a more affordable food choice compared to fats and proteins.

Now I am sure you have heard the term simple carbohydrates and complex carbohydrates, I hear people talk about this a lot within the fitness industry and to be honest it is old science. The best way to look at carbohydrates is using these two categories

Man Made Carbohydrates

Man made carbohydrates are any thing that WE have created unnaturally a sub-group typically made up of short chains and usually digested quickly within the body indicating a rapid release of

Sugars.

Man Made Carbohydrates are more commonly found in western diets where processed and refined foods are more available and as such are a large contributing factor to weight gain and retention.

Examples include:

All desserts (other than whole fruit), ice cream, sherbet, frozen yoghurt, most breads, many crackers, cakes, muffins, pancakes, waffles, pies, sweets, chocolate (dark, milk and white), breaded or battered foods, all types of dough (filo, pie crust), cereals, most pastas, noodles and couscous, jellies, jams and preserves, bagels, pretzels, pizza, peanut butter containing sweeteners, puddings and custards, crisps, granola bars, power bars, energy bars, most rice and corn cakes, fried vegetable snacks, ketchup, sweetened yoghurts and other sweetened dairy products, honey-roasted nuts, fizzy drinks.

Looking at the above, what stands out?

....

....

How many of the above do you have on a daily basis?

....

....

What could you do to remove simple carbohydrates from your diet?

....

....

Nature Made Carbohydrates

Natures made carbohydrates grow from the ground they are not
processed and contain high levels of fibre, remember that fibrous
carbohydrates do not effect blood sugar levels.

Examples include:

Fresh or frozen unsweetened fruits, all vegetables (other than white
potatoes) lettuce, cucumber, tomatoes, celery, spinach, peppers and
anything else which is naturally grown.

Think

Looking at the above, what stands out?

....

How many of the above do you have on a daily basis?

....

What action could you take today to introduce more Mothers
Natures Carbohydrates into your life?

....

Which Carbohydrate Is Better?

Hopefully, you will have noticed from the examples above that there is one clear distinction between man-made and nature made carbohydrates. Man made carbohydrates are most likely to be found in manufactured and highly processed foods whereas nature made carbohydrates are most likely to be found in foods that have remained close to their natural state (i.e. the way they were grown).

This makes nature made carbohydrates the better choice for those looking to control insulin levels (slower energy release prevents insulin spikes) or anyone embarking on a weight loss journey. Both types have a purpose and it's unlikely that you will go completely without one or the other but the slower release of energy provided by Mother natures carbohydrates helps to keep hunger at bay by creating a satisfying feeling of being 'full' for longer.

Task: Make it a conscious decision to choose ingredients that have remained close to their natural state and you won't go far wrong. When creating your shopping list, refer back to the Mother natures carbohydrates mentioned above and try to replace processed Man made carbohydrates with more natural carbohydrate options.

What Are Proteins?

Proteins are extremely complex and in reality there are only a few relevant things you need to know at this stage. Firstly, proteins are made up of amino acids which are the building blocks for all of the body's tissue. Your physiological proteins consist of 20 different amino acids and although your body requires all of them, you only have the ability to synthesise some of them. The remainder, those your body can't manufacture, must be sourced from the foods in your diet or you run the risk of developing a protein deficiency.

Current recommendations state that to meet your body's protein needs, you must consume a minimum of 0.8 grams of high quality protein per each kilogram of your bodyweight (or 0.4 grams per pound) per day. This is considered adequate in terms of meeting your essential amino acid requirements and it's an interesting fact, but really there is no need for the majority of people to consciously manage their protein intake in this way.

Secondly, protein is found mainly in animal products so meat is the primary source unless you are vegetarian. Glucose can also be found in protein sources but due to the longer breakdown period required, carbohydrates remain the body's main source of energy.

Examples of High Quality Protein Foods:

Soya beans, cheese, venison, skinless chicken breast, skinless turkey breast, boneless salmon fillets, sardines, beef fillet, lamb steak, pork chops, crab meat, cod, shrimp, haddock, bacon, pork sausages, eggs, goji berries, cottage cheese, houmous, yoghurt, broccoli, coconut, quinoa, most quorn products, green peas, nuts and nut butter, beans including black, white, pinto, chickpeas, tempeh, tofu, edamame (soybean still in the pod), leafy greens, hemp, chia seeds, sesame, sunflower and poppy seeds.

Looking at the above list, what immediately stands out to you?

....

....

How many of the high protein foods listed do you consume on a daily basis?

....

....

How do you currently get sufficient protein?

....

....

Your protein, as far as we are concerned, should come from natural (notice the trend on words) ingredients. So, although a chicken dipper contains a chicken of sorts, it shouldn't be considered a suitable source of high quality protein. The same applies to the following:

Corned beef, prosciutto, salami, supermarket bacon, hot dogs, mortadella, turkey dinosaurs etc.

The Lowdown On Meat Based Proteins

I'm a meat lover to so I'm not trying to say go vegetarian or vegan, but what I am saying is there are some real concerns about eating meat in general and eating too much meat, no matter how good it is.

Here are a few of my concerns about eating meat in general or eating too much meat, which is extremely common. First of all most of the meat which is commercially farmed here in the UK is well known to be treated with antibiotics, veterinary drugs and steroids, which is one of the very strong arguments about the antibiotic resistance problems we are facing, we are effectively getting over exposed to those drugs through the meat we are eating.

Many people who I have coached who are gluten sensitive say they often have a reaction to eating meat which has been fed on lots of grains (specifically gluten containing grains). Anybody who has been on a gluten free diet for some length of time and feels like they are not having a good response, could try cutting out any flesh foods that have been fed any kind of grains and often that is the missing element that will make a big difference in your life.

Unethical farming practices are also a big concern, remember for every £ you spend on their meats, you are funding these unethical farming practices. These animals are often raised in very tight quarters, stand, live and eat in their own urine and faeces. Imagine what your life would be like and then imagine what kind of an emotional state the animal would be in. Remember that emotions are a form of energy and those types of vibrations can (and do) get trapped within the flesh of the animal you eat.

Meat is by far the most toxic thing that goes into most people's mouths when it comes to diet, so when people ask me *"Dan, how can I eat healthy on my budget?"* I tell them if you have limited funds always spend your money on the highest quality meat you can get.

Organic, free range meat and not what I call fake free range, where they just let the cows run around for the last few days. Equally, when they say it's organic but feed them grains to fatten them up, then stop feeding them grains for the last 90 days.

I'm talking about buying meat raised by farmers who understand meat and animals and most importantly respect the animals. If you have to, do a little research on your own by phoning up suppliers, ask the farmers, ask the vendors and when you go to the shops ask where the meat comes from? Contact them and ask pointed questions.

There can be very high quality meat available by local farmers who are not certified organic but do not use chemicals. So your best place to go looking for that, is at farmers markets and I've seen lots of great stuff!

"Eat the highest quality meat you can, even if you have a low budget, always seek the best you can get with the money you can afford." Paul Chek

What Are Fats?

Firstly, let's bust the myth that fats are bad. Sure some fats are bad and most modern 'known' fats come into this category, but there are also good fats and it's essential that we get enough of them in our diet, as a diet too low in fat can lead to skin problems, inhibit the body's control of inflammation and adversely affect blood pressure. Basically, there are two groups of fats you need to know about:

1. Saturated Fats

These are the bad fats associated with heart disease and known to be detrimental to overall health. Common sources are meat fat, butter and processed foods such as cakes and biscuits.

2. Unsaturated Fats

These can be split into two further groups:

Monounsaturated fats – these are the good fats known to be of benefit to overall health. Common sources are oils such as olive, groundnut and rapeseed and they're also found in seeds and nuts.

Polyunsaturated fats – these also have positive health benefits in that they can help to lower unhealthy blood cholesterol levels. Polyunsaturated fats are also important in that they contain essential fatty acids, which the body can't produce by itself. However, it's now known that they may also reduce healthy levels of blood cholesterol so a combination of polyunsaturated and monounsaturated fats are needed in the diet to achieve a healthy balance. Common sources are vegetable fats and oily fish.

The Bad Fats

The fats to eat sparingly or to avoid altogether in your diet are saturated fats and trans fatty acids. Both are linked with raised cholesterol levels, clogged arteries, and an increased risk of developing heart disease.

Saturated fats are found in animal products and the common sources mentioned above.

The Good Fats

Both mono and polyunsaturated fats, when eaten in moderation can help to lower cholesterol levels and reduce your risk of developing heart disease.

Monounsaturated fats form a large part of the diet in Mediterranean countries (olive oil in particular) and this is thought to be the reason for low levels of heart disease in these areas. Typically liquid at room temperature but solid when refrigerated, these heart-healthy fats are a good source of vitamin E, a health-boosting antioxidant which is often lacking in our diets, and can be found in olives, avocados, hazelnuts, almonds, brazil nuts, cashews, sesame seeds, pumpkin seeds, and olive, canola and peanut oils.

Much heralded omega-3 fatty acids are one type of polyunsaturated fat, found in fish (salmon, trout, catfish, mackerel), as well as flaxseed and walnuts. Oily fish contains the 'long-chain' type of omega-3s, which are known to be particularly effective in terms of lowering the potential to develop heart disease.

Task: Remove all cooking oils made from animal fats and all 'fake' fats from your kitchen.

There is evidence to back up claims that saturated fats can increase the risk of developing colon and prostate cancers so we recommend, whenever possible, choosing healthy unsaturated fats and consciously striving to achieve and maintain a healthy weight.

We also hear a great deal about trans-fatty acids or trans-fats these days but it's important to be aware that there are two types: the naturally occurring type found in small amounts in dairy and meat and the artificial type, found in liquid oils that are hardened/ processed into 'partially hydrogenated' fats. The naturally occurring types are not of particular concern, especially if you choose low-fat dairy products and lean meats, but the artificial types should be avoided. They're used extensively in frying and found in baked goods, biscuits, icings, crackers, packaged snack foods, microwave popcorn, and some varieties of margarine.

Examples of Good Fats:

Olive oil, coconut oil, canola oil, peanut oil, sesame oil, avocados, olives, nuts (almonds, brazil nuts, peanuts (unsalted), macadamia nuts, hazelnuts, pecans, cashews), peanut butter, soybean oil, corn oil, sunflower oil, walnuts, sunflower, sesame, and pumpkin seeds, flaxseed, fatty fish (salmon, tuna, mackerel, herring, trout, sardines)

What is apparent to you having looked at the good fats listed above?

....

....

What bad fats do you have at home?

....

....

Why would now be a good time to throw them away?

....

....

It's unlikely that you will be able to remove all 'bad' fats from your diet completely but you should still be consciously aware of what you're eating at all times. Pay attention to what's in the foods you eat at home as well as when you're eating out or grabbing a bite on the go. Take note - fats are very good at being hidden.

WARNING: avoid the temptation to buy anything with 'light',

'reduced fat', 'low calorie', 'low fat' or anything else suggesting a food represents a healthier option. Anything with a FAT WARNING on the label probably wasn't good enough to eat in the first place.

Stimulants

For me, stimulants are anything you consume to cause a rapid change in the natural production and release of chemicals within the body – a sugar rush, a caffeine boost, a legal high if you like. These sorts of stimulants have become commonplace over recent years with a well-known 'energy drink' and a plethora of coffee shop chains leading the trend. As I see it, socially accepted stimulants are just as bad as the not so social and illegal varieties, yet they don't get the same bad press. However, the fact remains that in effect they are all potentially damaging to health, and here's why…

> The long-term effects are still unknown; especially with unnatural stimulants which increase the chemical content within the body.
>
> The mid-term effects are known to be health related issues and illnesses, not forgetting they are addictive.
>
> The short-term effects are a change in the way the body functions.

The most common socially accepted stimulants are as follows:

Sugar: If your goal is to lose weight and remain healthy then you need to take note of this. You will have to remove 'fake' sugars from over 80% of your diet. Now, I'd like to say 'remove *all* fake sugar' but this is highly unrealistic and hard to manage unless you have the time and you feel really serious about adopting a RAW style diet (ideal but sometimes not practical).

Salt: Like fats, there are different types of salts to be considered;

there are the good and the bad. The good are those found in plants and the sea – these contain healthy minerals and offer the same taste value as the bad salts. For example, Himalayan Rock Salt is a pure, hand-mined salt that's derived from ancient sea salt deposits and is believed to be the purest form of salt available. The salt crystals range in colour from white to varying shades of pink and deep reds, the result of a high mineral and iron content. The bad salts are the processed varieties, therefore most table salts. Table salt is typically mined from underground salt deposits and heavily processed to eliminate minerals, with most varieties containing an additive to prevent clumping. Salt causes a mixed message to be sent to the brain as it's dehydrating but also sends signals of hunger.

Caffeine: I love my coffee, so I'm writing this with great care to avoid sounding hypocritical. Caffeine is *the* high drink and it has become one of the most readily accepted means of socialising on a daily basis. We all know the 'caffeine kick' effect but what most fail to realise is that over consumption is counterproductive. The effects are short-lived and actually inhibit the release of naturally occurring chemicals, meaning the end result is similar to the highs and lows of sugar spikes and crashes. Of course, coffee alone is not the only issue. Added extras such as sugar, syrup and milk all add to the problem – most of which go unnoticed or are forgotten about.

Alcohol: Again, I also enjoy the occasional Jack Daniels but as far as the body is concerned, alcohol is a sugar, thereby a stimulant and inhibitor. Alcohol reduces the body's ability to absorb minerals and nutrients, it plays with the body's thermostat, and it also causes insulin spikes, thereby generating fat storage. This means that as far as weight loss is concerned it simply doesn't help, actually reducing the speed at which fat is digested and removed from the body.

Tobacco: Nothing positive can be said about the consumption of tobacco. The effects on the body are horrific and the effect it has on weight loss and gain are dramatic. If you smoke, now is the time to stop. However, it's important to avoid the temptation to opt for some form of substitute that will replicate the effects. If you stop and you feel the need to hold something, opt for a carrot. If you need a break out of the office, make a fruit tea, and if you need a replacement, be aware that patches and all other forms of fake cigarette are still bad for your health, despite the positive packaging and marketing.

Task

1.   Remove 'fake' salts from your diet and throw away all table salts from your cupboards. Replace them with natural organic varieties, but still use sparingly. These can be ordered online or picked up from local health food stores, but always check to make sure they don't have any additives included.

2.   Over the coming weeks, reduce any caffeine consumption to the minimum. For example, one coffee per day. It will take seven days to re-set, restore and kick-start the natural production on inhibited chemicals in your body. Avoid the temptation to reach for energy drinks and allow your body to regain control.

3.   If you have no intention of cutting out alcohol completely, then reduce your consumption to about six units per week, aiming to then cut to five, then to four units.

4.   Stop smoking: go cold turkey. The lengthening of life, not to mention the financial saving, should be enough for anyone to seriously act right now.

Nutrition – You Are What You Eat

It's time you started thinking for yourself and stopped accepting the past as guidance for the future.

Mass society teaches/educates us that everything must go through a process before it can be consumed hence the reason why more space is allocated to packaged items than fresh produce in our supermarkets. This accepted view needs to be changed and a more positive 'shopping focus' put in place. Another positive shift in thinking is to let go of the belief that a 'real' meal has to be served hot.

Do You Need Organic/Raw?

My own diet is varied and where possible I attempt to consume at least 90% organic foods. The organic food diet was alien to me at first, as with many people, and psychologically it offered many challenges. But the more I began to uncover the dynamics and science of how food is digested, the more I accepted that this was a solution offering everything my previous diet had been lacking.

There are many good reasons to eat organic foods and there are also good reasons to reduce the amount of food you cook. I'm not saying you should eat everything raw but the nutritional benefits it brings include aiding weight loss and the repairing of your body.

Eating quality food is great, but preparing it to get the maximum nutritional return is what really counts.

The organic raw food principle in a nutshell (pun intended!): in the majority of cases, cooking a food decreases its nutritional value. As an example, vitamin C is destroyed by heat and the cancer-fighting properties of green vegetables such as broccoli are greatly diminished through cooking. It's for this reason that the bulk of a raw food diet is consumed in its raw state, and where cooking is required, temperatures remain below 48 degrees Celsius (118 degrees Fahrenheit) and ideally below 40 degrees Celsius (104 degrees Fahrenheit) to prevent heat damage and therefore preserve as much of the nutrient value as possible.

Think About This For A Moment …

Visualise the journey a baked potato makes from field to fork. It begins in the ground, covered in earth and packed full of energy. It's uprooted and begins its journey to the consumer. I'm unsure of the exact number of days it may be in transit or storage before making it to a shop shelf, and then the number of days it takes to journey from the shop shelf into a kitchen cupboard or fridge needs to be considered, let alone the time it may languish there before being used. The cooking process usually involves being baked in an oven at temperatures far greater than 40 degrees C to ensure the skin becomes dry and crispy before then smothering it in saturated fats to add moisture before consumption. Your body attempts to break down and extract any remaining nutrients but ultimately struggles due to the negative 'value' overload.

I know this is a slightly dramatic and overly simplified account of a baked potato's journey but the point I want to demonstrate is that sourcing any produce in its rawest of forms (dirt and all) and using it as quickly as possible in the rawest consumable way possible ensures the quality of the produce is transferred and fully utilised. Sure, a baked potato isn't a baked potato unless it goes through the baking process, however this diet is not about eliminating essentially nutrient-dense foods from your diet, it's about understanding how altering the way you source and prepare food ultimately holds the key to getting the most nutritional value from the foods you eat.

I can guarantee that there is nothing more enjoyable than sitting down and eating something you have constructed and produced from scratch.

Food through new eyes – not something needed just to survive but something that creates a life worth living.

What changes can you make to your shopping habits?

....

....

Where can you source quality raw food?

....

....

Frozen Vs Fresh

Let The Debate Commence ...

There is no question that if you are able to source fresh produce then there really is no better option, however the fact remains that some ingredients are simply not geographically or physically possible to obtain fresh from source so rather than removing them completely from your diet, settling for frozen is the next best option.

In situations where you are unable to go directly to source, or foods are so far removed from being fresh after travelling thousands of miles over several days or perhaps weeks, then I would prefer to opt for the frozen version, especially if frozen at source. Why? As a general rule of thumb, fruits picked for freezing are usually processed prior to ripening, and, as this is when they usually display the peak level of nutritional value, the frozen version therefore represents a better choice than the 'fresh' version languishing on a supermarket shelf.

Of course, there are mixed opinions on this subject and the debate will no doubt rumble on and continue to waste more energy than needed, but let's just use the sweet potato as an example. I am fortunate to have a farm shop less than a few miles from my home and I know that the sweet potatoes sold there are certainly sourced from within a reasonable distance of the shop and 100% from within the UK. However, a quick look at the prepackaged options available in most of the larger grocery stores nationwide will reveal that many varieties are imported.

It makes perfect sense to buy as fresh as possible. When foods are exposed to excessive heat and light after being uprooted from their natural state, the nutrients begin to degrade significantly, especially vitamin C and thiamin (vitamin B), which are particularly delicate. The balance therefore becomes a matter of limiting the number of degenerative processes in order to maintain the highest possible nutrient value.

Preparing the Feast – Eye Candy?

Sometimes more can be said for the way something looks than the way it tastes. If it looks good then the likelihood is it will taste good, or at least that's what the mind is attempting to process (via its senses), and this is exactly the tactic employed by marketing companies on food packaging. Ask yourself this: when was the last time a packaged meal actually turned out looking like it did on the packet? I'm pretty sure the answer is NEVER, and the reason for this is simple – it can't.

The first time I went into a wholefood store, the vibrant colours that glared back at me blinded me. This is a statement that can only be made subject to your past learnings. Let me explain: the mind, seeing something bright in colour, will associate what it sees with certain beliefs usually installed back in childhood. This can then go two ways, depending entirely on your childhood experiences of brightly coloured foods. If bright equated to good in your childhood, your mind will see vibrant foods as good foods, but if bright equated to bad in your childhood, your mind will see vibrant foods as bad foods.

For many years, food for me was something I needed to survive, not something I felt particularly inspired to spend any time on. I was fortunate with the foods I was given in my childhood, but eating food was still only considered to be a necessity and not an enjoyable part of life. Having fun with the colours you have available is essential, not only in your own food preparation but also in terms of showing others, the younger generations included, that **food = fun.**

The more we educate ourselves and others on food production and evolution, the more able we are to use food to our advantage and to create a strong respectful connection to the benefits.

How can you improve the quality of the preparation?

....

....

What value do you attach to food?

....

....

In what ways have your food choices changed since starting the book?

....

....

Is Fresh the Solution?

The more appetising a food looks the more likely you are to eat it. Just think for a moment about the vast number of fast food outlets and the pictures they display of the 'meal deals' they have on offer – how often does the actual product look anything like the picture?

Rarely: and if it did, I'd question the level of synthetic content required to create such an appearance.

The truth is that we primarily gauge our food choices on the visual representation along with the smell. It's only once we have satisfied these criteria that we consider the taste and texture. By using a hidden creative ability that we all have, we can think about preparing food as if preparing the paint to create a masterpiece.

So, let's quickly summarise the nutritionally rich foods you *can* eat at this point before you slip into focusing on what you *can't* eat.

Nutritionally rich foods generally fall into the following factors.

• Foods that represent their original state – be aware of products that have been refined to improve their appearance (wax on certain fruits for example).

• Foods that do not have any additional artificial flavours or colourings – this is because naturally nutritious foods don't need to have anything added to them.

• Foods that are not packaged in a way to stop them from breaking down or following their own natural cycle - if it's rotten then it's rotten, simple.

• Foods that have only one ingredient – a carrot is a carrot, no other ingredients should be listed.

• Foods that don't have any sugars or refined white/bleached chemicals added – this is because they are good enough on their own.

The following foods are now staples in my own diet:

• Salad vegetables, such as cucumbers and red onion
• Salad toppings, such as olives
• Garlic
• Avocados

- LOTS of cannellini beans
- LOTS of lentils
- Other varieties of beans
- Brown rice
- Quinoa
- Raisins
- Almond milk
- Tofu
- Canned tomatoes, crushed or diced
- Frozen fruit
- Frozen vegetables
- Balsamic vinegar
- Nutritional yeast
- Spices – curry powder, seasoning, chili powder, etc.

The basic diet consists of nuts, seeds, fruit, vegetables, olive oil, coconut oil, herbs and spices, plant based proteins, organic lean meat proteins and as the sample recipes on the following pages demonstrate, the seemingly limited food choices in no way limit the potential to create delicious and nutritious meals.

Getting Back to the Basics of Living ...

If You Can't Pronounce It You Shouldn't Be Eating It

I think that by stripping back the ingredients to the rawest possible form, you not only simplify the overall process, you also make it much simpler to tailor your consumption needs to the type of lifestyle you live.

The basic concept with all nutrition is that you are simply a by-product of what you eat. The more time you spend re-educating yourself in terms of looking into which foods will support you in the best way possible, the more you make it possible to become a better version of yourself – the best version it's possible to be.

Why wouldn't you be the best you can be?

....

....

Why would you settle for anything less than great in life?

....

....

With nutrition, you have to ask yourself what is truly important: are you likely to love a better, healthier life consuming good, nutritionally rich foods, or a life plagued with illness and poison? This may seem like an overly stark comparison but the reality is that the more basic you become with your diet the better and healthier it's likely to be.

"If you continue to eat unhealthy foods and keep gaining Fat, you are in affect playing Russian roulette with your life and eventually that bullet will come and bite you in the bum ... Hard"

To really get back to basics, it's a good idea to adopt a 'baby mind'. When we are young, our vocabulary is limited and as we grow it expands and grows accordingly. In terms of diet, the more we grow the more experiences we gain of colours, tastes and textures so our food vocabulary also becomes more varied and colourful. When you use your baby mind, you go back to thinking about the words a baby might use to describe the food they want. In most cases, the foods a baby is aware of are healthy choices, and although limited, they represent foods that promote healthy living. It's only when we become adults that our mind takes on a belief structure of trusting others to provide truthful facts about the contents of food products and we trust that foods will not be labelled in such a way that any negative aspects are deliberately hidden from us as the consumer.

'Baby mind' foods might include: apple, peach, carrot, juice etc. After all, it's very unlikely that a baby would request a microwave meal topped with extra cheese and a side order of fries, isn't it?

On the subject of children, I make a very conscious effort as a parent and uncle to impartially educate children on the rights and wrongs of the world. One afternoon, while we were having a BBQ, a friend made a point of offering to take the children to a well-known fast food outlet for burgers, chips and a toy if they behaved. My nephew, Joseph (aged 9), confidently announced, "Shouldn't we be going somewhere that offers good food to reward us, not processed junk?"

Sure, it's fair to say that this way of thinking isn't the norm and, in fact, the majority of adults present laughed, but it's also fair to say that Joseph made a valid point. Within our culture we are taught that cake, chocolate and all things high in saturated fat are indeed a treat.

From this point forward change your thinking – think 'baby mind'.

Kitchen Basics

Okay, so what about the kitchen basics you'll need to make the most of your new and supportive diet! Remember, there's nothing complicated about the foods you'll be eating so there's no need for any complicated kitchen gadgetry.

There's every chance that everything you need is already in your kitchen. The basics are:

Knife – you'll need a sharp knife that can be used to chop everything from a pineapple to a bunch of fresh herbs. Make sure it can be cleaned and sharpened easily.

Chopping board – you'll need a quality board that will allow you to chop a wide variety of vegetables and fresh ingredients safely and easily. There are plenty of different styles and brands on the market so it comes down to personal choice. Fans of wooden boards believe wood has antibacterial properties and it won't dull your knife as quickly as plastic, but fans of plastic believe that being able to put your chopping board in the dishwasher makes it the most convenient option.

Measuring tools – you'll need a means of measuring out ingredients when following recipes. There are lots of simple and inexpensive options available in shops or you can just use utensils you already have in your kitchen. The key is to have designating measuring tools that will allow you to be consistent with your measurements.

Scrubbing brush – you'll need a brush that's robust enough to allow you to scrub soil etc. from fresh produce.

Blender – I would advise you to buy a good blender nutri-bullets are great for making fresh fruit smoothies etc.

The First Step

Like any new adventure, it can be both challenging and daunting when you begin looking for solutions, especially if you are the only one taking this path. Personally, I have found that you will meet two different types of people along the way: Those who are interested and wish you luck, or those who will laugh in your face – literally. To overcome these minor confrontations, simply remember the deeper reason behind what you are planning to do and remind yourself of the long-term benefits of doing what you are doing.

Why are you improving your dietary habits?

....

....

Why is now the right time to change for the better?

....

....

What excuses have you made in the past?

....

....

Getting started at the shop is going to be easier than you think.

When I first started, I was keen to clear out the old and introduce the new, but the truth is that if you have been eating a relatively balanced diet then there is little that will go to waste. Sure, there are going to be lots of new and exciting additions but, overall, the changes are not as vast as one might assume.

On the topic of getting started, avoid making the assumption that it is going to be more expensive to eat raw foods or a diet consisting mainly of organic related produce. This is not actually true as eating more of the 'good stuff' is actually more cost effective in the majority of cases, even when organic produce is the primary choice. Sure, choosing organic varieties of everything may increase your costs depending on your location, but with a little research and perhaps organising a monthly rather than weekly shop, you can justify travelling slightly further afield to find better value in farm shops or farmers' markets. For example: I usually travel 10 miles to a rural farm shop to source all vegetables. These are bought in five and 10 kilo bags with a 10 kilo bag of carrots currently costing just under £3.00. Compare this to the £1.75 I'd need to pay for just one kilo in my local supermarket and that's a whopping saving of £14.50 in just one product.

Get Local

As previously mentioned, the closer you are to the source the finer the nutritional content, and as my own experiences show, costs can also be significantly reduced. Personally, I believe that buying locally is a winner all around, and better than so-called organics that are being imported from around the world. Investing in your local farmers allows them to invest in better farming methods and thus create a healthier product. I know that a visit to your local farmer may not be your solution but, where possible, always buy local.

Once you have sourced your 'natural consumables', it's time to look at the things that are simply unavailable locally. In the absence of a local health food store, the Internet offers a useful substitute, and once you have established a regular shopping list, costs can be lowered by buying in bulk. However, if you do have a natural/ health food shop in your area that doesn't appear to stock the items you want, don't be afraid to ask because they may be willing to buy them in for you.

Dan Aguilera

Chapter Three

"I can safely say that UU has become a part of my every day life for the better. You are worth your weight in gold 10 times over. Not just for pushing me to do what you know I can but for helping me through tough times too and always catching up with me if you think something isn't quite right. You both dedicate all your time and passion into what you do and all the love for it is spread out throughout the sessions and that's what really motivates us to keep on going. I wouldn't give it up for the world now and can't wait to start seeing results again!" Ellen G.

What Is The Metabolic Rate?

We hear a lot about metabolism—and often blame our "slow metabolism" for our inability to keep our weight under control. But what is metabolism, exactly? And is there anything we can do to change our metabolic rate?

Our metabolic rate is the rate at which our body burns calories. Many people understand the metabolic rate to be a major factor in determining how quickly or how easily they can lose weight, but along with this understanding comes the potential for a great deal of misunderstanding as people find themselves confused with conflicting advice and theories. People say to me all of the time that they believe they are overweight because they have a slow metabolism and that their friend can eat what they like and never put on weight. It's because of this that I recommend you take your time over the next section to ensure you fully digest and understand what is being said. If you need to, fold over this page and refer back to it over the coming days.

Gaining this knowledge is a very important element of getting things right in terms of maintaining a healthy body and being able to control your weight. However, you might be tempted to flick past it, so it's my intention to give you just enough information to be of benefit without giving you too much and switching you off as a consequence.

It Is Important...

THE BASICS – Metabolism basically refers to all the chemical processes that take place in the body in order to sustain life– such as breathing, maintenance of heat, heartbeat, blood circulation, and the activities of the nervous system and internal organs to keep your brain functioning and extract energy from your food.

When you hear the term *metabolic rate*–more accurately called *basal* (or *resting*) *metabolic rate*–that refers to the number of calories your body at rest uses each day, just to keep all your vital organs functioning.

Once we go beyond these functions we burn additional calories through your daily activities such as walking, climbing stairs, exercising, playing sport, even just carrying the shopping, but by far, the majority of the calories that you burn each day are your basal calories.

The number of calories that you burn every day is directly related to your body composition. Think of your body as divided into two compartments. In one compartment is all the body fat; in the other compartment is everything that isn't fat (e.g., bone, fluid, tissue, muscle)–that's the fat-free compartment. The size of your fat-free compartment determines your metabolic rate, with every pound of fat-free mass burning about 14 calories per day.

If you weigh 150 pounds and 50 pounds of you is fat and 100 pounds is fat-free, then you would burn about 1,400 calories per day at rest. If you don't get much activity, you won't burn much more than this throughout the day. But if you weigh 150 pounds and 25 pounds of you is fat, and 125 pounds of you is fat free, then you burn 1,750 calories per day at rest. And if you get some regular exercise and burn a few hundred calories more per day, your total calorie burn for the day might be 2,000 calories!

Since the fat-free compartment contains muscle tissue, one of the best things you can do to boost your metabolic rate is to strength-train to increase your muscle mass. If you build up 10 pounds of lean body mass, that's another 500 extra calories that you burn per day—not to mention the calories that you burn through exercise.

The first little fact we need to consider here is not the main deal, but it's interesting. Most dieticians seem to agree that one pound of fat is about equivalent to 3500 calories of stored energy – that's about 7500 calories per kilo. If you can reduce your calorie intake to 1000 less than your recommended daily allowance you will potentially lose 1000 calories of body fat a day, or about two pounds/one kilo a week.

The trouble with this is that in most cases, and from my vast knowledge of dealing with people in real life and not from a textbook, your body is just too efficient and it simply slows down your metabolic rate to meet the level of calorie intake. This means that in most cases dieting slows your metabolism, which leads to having less personal energy, lower concentration levels, and everything becoming a chore, as you just don't feel good.

On the other hand, a high metabolic rate or 'fast' metabolism leads to feeling that you have energy to do everything. This can of course make a huge difference to the way you live your life. Our current lifestyle of fast foods and convenience foods can fool us into believing we are eating lots but there is very little nutrition getting down to the cells of our body so it believes we are starving and consequently slows our metabolic rate right down.

If we are going to reverse this, we need to ensure that our body is getting all the nutrition it needs at a cellular level. Once we've done this, we can drop the calorie intake and our metabolic rate will stay high. However, we have further problems in that the food available to us on supermarket shelves is grown in nutrient deficient soils, picked green so it ships well, stored for too long, and if it's pre-packaged it's normally over-processed. There just isn't enough nutrition in our food to sustain us, and if we look at botanical factors and the active ingredients in our food with things like the amino acids then we are in real trouble.

For the energy equation to be transferred into weight change i.e. the food we eat less the energy we burn equalling net gain or net loss in daily energy, we need to provide our body with all the nutrition it needs on a daily basis so that it doesn't fight against starvation by slowing down our metabolic rate. Something else to realise is that weight gained through a slower metabolism is most likely going to be stored on hips, thighs and stomach.

In summary, if someone has told you that a diet means removing calories, they are wrong. What they should be saying is that it means improving the *quality* of the calories you consume. **Slowing down your metabolic rate does not and will not support a healthy lifestyle.**

The Power Of Muscle

Would it to be fair to say that most people have a small amount of muscle surrounded by a large amount of fat within their problem areas?

Now what we want to actually do is have a larger amount of muscle surrounded by a smaller amount of fat, therefore giving us toned up look we are after.

Now this is called the power of muscle, for every 1lb of muscle we can put on you or reactivate on your body you will burn an extra 50 calories extra per day. So if we can put 5kg of muscle on you then you will burn an extra 550 calories per day, which sounds awesome.

However, you are probably reading this now, thinking like most people I work with that you would like to burn the extra 550 calories per day – "but actually Dan I want to lose weight, I don't want to gain a stone of muscle and be walking around all muscular, it's not really the look most people want."

It doesn't work like that because 1lb of muscle is about the same size as a large strawberry and 1lb of fat is the size of a large block of butter, so if I said to you now -let's remove the equivalent fat of 10 blocks of butter from your waist, hips or bum and replace it with 10 large strawberries, you would be over the moon! You might weigh the same on the scales but your body shape would change considerably which is the key thing.

That being said one of my biggest frustrations in the fitness industry is that trainers say to clients that you haven't lost any weight this week! You must have gained muscle....

Heard that before?

It's actually a copout, the reason being is that it's really hard to gain muscle, even the top natural bodybuilders in the world will only gain around 8-10lbs of muscle per year.

You are never going to realistically exercise to the intensity of a body builder and start to gain muscle. So if anybody says to you that you haven't lost weight because you have gained muscle, it's a copout.

The key thing to getting the extra calorific burn is something called muscle activation. Let me explain this to you. Let's say for example you have 20lbs of muscle in your legs but due to what you currently do on a daily basis, you probably aren't using all of that muscle. You are probably only using a portion of that and let's say as an example that you are only using 2lbs of it. If you are only using 2lbs active then you will only burn 100 calories per day because every 1lb of active muscle you have you will burn 50 calories, so 2lbs = 100calories. Our job with the exercise is to start to activate as much of that muscle as we can. For example, if over a period of time we can activate all 20lbs of the muscle you will burn 1000 calories per day. Now you already have this muscle on you in terms of weight, you just need to get it active and working for you because the more active muscle you have, the more calories you will burn at rest and therefore the more fat you are going to burn on a daily basis.

Exercise - The Power Behind Fat Loss

Now when most people try and lose weight, get fit and healthy, they normally go and join a gym.

Have you been a member of a gym before?

Now typically when you go and join a gym the membership adviser will sell you the membership and then get you booked in with the fitness instructor to write you a weight loss program.

Now I've been really fortunate to have visited hundreds of gyms around the world and even more fortunate to be able to assess what we are doing as an industry in terms of our exercise prescription. Unfortunately we are doing really poor, it doesn't matter if you are joining for weight loss, toning, sports specific, muscle building, fitness or injury rehabilitation the same program is written for everyone and it typically looks like this; you are going to warm up on the bike for 5 minutes, then go on the treadmill for 10 minutes, the cross trainer for 10 minutes, maybe the rower or the stepper for 10 minutes, do a few weights, a few crunches or Ab work, stretch and leave.

Sound familiar?

If you train this way then your calorie burn off is only 2 hours, which means that you are burning calories for 2 hours after your workout. If you do what we call interval training where you are going hard, easy, hard, easy, hard, easy your calorie burn off will be 7 hours after, so you have boosted your metabolism up to burn calories for longer. Now what I do with my clients at Ultimate U Fitness is interval training resistance and cardio, all put together in a particular way, with certain reps, sets, tempo, time under tension, pre extortion of muscle groups, something called blood pooling and all this fancy scientific stuff that you needn't worry about right now. Basically with my clients, their calorie burn off is up to 72 hours after the workout. So 72 hours after the workout they are still burning fat, which is why the results I get are so good.

Now even if you get this bit right, this is where most people fail with regards to exercise and fat loss. It takes 29 minutes of high intensity cardio training to burn something called muscle glycogen (the sugar in your muscles) you cannot burn fat until you have burnt all of this sugar. Imagine we have 2 pots, the first pot is the muscle glycogen and the second pot is the fat pot. So for 30 minutes high intensity cardio, you are only burning fat for 1 minute, it takes 29 minutes of high intensity cardio to burn all of the sugar in pot 1 before you burn fat. If I get you to sprint on a treadmill for 30 minutes, you will only be burning fat for 1 minute, which is why most people in the gym using the cardio equipment, really do not get to burn fat and therefore generally do not change shape.

Here is the key thing; it takes 3-4 minutes of high intensity resistance training to burn the muscle glycogen. Therefore after 3-4 minutes of the resistance based exercise you have burnt that sugar pot, therefore you can go into the second pot which is the fat pot and burn the fat for the remainder of the session. Now that has got to be put together in a certain way, like I said earlier with certain reps, sets, tempo etc. You cannot just stand there and do some bicep curls for 3-4 minutes and expect to burn all of the sugar in the muscle, it has got to be structured in a certain way.

You only have a window of 45 minutes, after 45 minutes of exercise women stop producing oestrogen and men stop burning testosterone, which means after that period of time you will fall of the edge of the shelf and you can no longer metabolise fat as energy. The only thing you can burn is muscle, which is counterproductive for fat loss because the more muscle you have the more calories you burn at rest and you do not want to burn the muscle.

Ideally what you want to do is 3-4 minutes of muscle glycogen burning with 41 minutes fat burning. So not only will you get 41 minutes fat burning within the session, you will get 72 hours after the session, which is again why I get some amazing results with my clients.

There are some sample workouts for you later in the book for you to follow which will allow you to burn fat for the 41 minutes and the 72 hours after doing them. You can do these workouts at your own intensity and level, as you become fitter and stronger you will be able to push them to a higher intensity.

The Problem With the Way We Think

If you have tried dieting in the past and it hasn't worked for you, then it's likely that the deeper rooted issues were not addressed. Sure, cutting calories and exercising or trying the latest fad pill may have had some effect, but the chances are the weight has sprung back on in no time at all, right?

If this is you, then it's nothing to be ashamed of. You are like the many other millions of people around the world looking for a solution to a problem that they have identified, and for that alone you should congratulate yourself and be happy. Identification is the first step, knowledge the second, and action the third.

Reading this book is already improving your knowledge so let's look ahead to the mind and the thinking behind the actions stage.

"We not only become like those we mix with, but like those we think about the most."

The above is something I say a lot, and for one very good reason. What we think about becomes the way we communicate with ourselves internally and as a result is then projected into our behaviours.

Think fat and that's what you'll become…

FACT: more people start a diet for aesthetic reasons rather than lifestyle choices and their actions are usually driven by a celebrity or a large organisation promoting the idea for one reason only – to make money.

Although there is a degree of financial motivation involved in writing this book, my main aim is to share the knowledge I have so that I may help you to improve your life and make changes for the better. Sure, money helps but my main objective is to help you get results. It's for this reason that I ask one thing of you – question the motives behind those glossy adverts that show you rapid weight loss results in return for investing in a certain product and at the same time, question why obesity is an on-going and growing concern.

These 'mind-plays' have caused many misconceptions about food and they generalise people who adopt a certain way of living.

Think for a moment about what comes to mind when you read the following:

- Hippy
- Bodybuilder
- Vegan
- Pescetarian

Now think about how you perceive their environments – a hippy based environment, a bodybuilder's environment, vegan and pescetarian – what images are created in your mind; how do you see those people living, and what do their environments look like? Now think about the last time you saw an old picture of yourself and remember the way the image made you feel. Were you repulsed, upset, angry, lost for words?

What pictures did you create about yourself?

....

....

What didn't you like about those internal images?

....

....

Why is now the right time to change that perception forever?

....

....

What happens if you don't make the changes needed?

....

....

....

....

What we see internally generally manifests into external behaviour and creates a perception we act upon. Now let's pause for a moment and think long term. Think ahead to a moment in the future when you have achieved your ideal weight and imagine looking back at an image of yourself as you are now.

What would you say to yourself?

....

....

I ask you to do this because weight loss or dietary adjustments should be looked at as long term projects and with a slightly different objective to others you may have had in the past.

Dan Aguilera

Chapter Four

"Joining UU was the best fitness-related decision I have ever made. Since joining in August 2014, I am now fitter and stronger than I have ever been. I feel sad that I spent so many years being a member of various gyms and never actually achieving anything. But I'm here now and I'm not going anywhere! Dan has the knowledge, expertise, drive and enthusiasm that have helped me on my journey. 'Thank you' just isn't enough" - Kerry P-T.

Benefits Beyond Weight Loss

Approaching weight loss or diet with the sole goal of losing weight is never productive, nor is it healthy. Changing your approach to focus on the three areas of nutrition, fitness and lifestyle will bring mental, emotional and physical benefits that complement your whole life, not just the way you look. I've found that those who keep the weight off are those who choose to follow my overall lifestyle changes.

How much better would your life be if you were the weight you wanted to be and you didn't have to think about it ever again?

....

Aiming to be a healthy weight is different to aiming for weight loss. Being healthy incorporates every aspect of your future life, not just your body image and eliminates many other negative aspects of a poor diet such as bloating, skin conditions, lack of energy and low levels of concentration. The choice you make right now depends on the answers you give to these two questions:

1.   Do you actually want to lose weight?
2.   Why do you want to lose weight?

The answers to these questions generally indicate the 'value' factor involved in the overall process, or the mindful aspect of it all. It's also being able to give honest answers to these questions that will release you from the emotional shackles holding you back.

To start change you must first be open to change. For things to change, you must change

A Few Points to Get Started

Accept that you can be happy right now. With many things, there's often the temptation to wait until the timing is right or the universe is perfectly aligned to give you want you want before making a start. Sadly, and again having worked with many different people, the right time will usually end up being no time. When you start to shift from the 'then' to the 'now' you begin to free yourself up from past problems and future potential issues.

It's only by living in the moment that you can start to take action on the person you are right now and thus change the path you're likely to follow. Avoid the temptation to wait until some future date to make these changes to your life – take charge right now... now... now...

Why do I deserve to be happy and have everything I want in life?

....

....

Why haven't I done what I really wanted so far in my life?

....

....

Look at the reason *why*. To start with, you're not the only person with issues or bad past experiences or anything else negative so GET OVER IT. This may seem harsh but the reality is that the longer you live in the past, the longer you will be tormented with whatever negativity it had to offer. The root cause of weight gain for most people is a traumatic event that spiralled into comfort frenzy... and the rest is history.

Now, don't get me wrong, I know that things can be tough but how about choosing to deal with things differently. When times get tough, or you're hurt, or something negative happens, how about reaching for something positive that will assist you rather than reaching for the bar of chocolate? Just imagine for a moment what it would be like to reach out and ask for help (no shame in asking for help when you need it) rather than folding in and adding to the bad news by reaching for the bar of chocolate; what would happen if you actively chose to do something that would support you in a healthy and long-term positive way?

Why have I been holding on to past negative issues?

....

....

What comfort have they provided?

....

....

When would be the right time to let go?

....

....

Why haven't I let go in the past?

....

....

What will happen if I don't let go right now?

....

Next, you need to commit to being the person you want to be.
We all have choices in life; to have or to have not, to stand alone
and allow others to follow, or to become lost in the crowd and be
forgotten. With weight loss, as with any other kind of change, you

have to commit to making change happen. Without commitment, making changes in the areas of your life that need attention becomes impossible and you will never achieve the full life you want or the memories that go with it.

"The most difficult thing is the decision to act, the rest is merely tenacity." – Amelia Earhart

For me, commitment basically means to follow through on what you said you would do. Being able to commit also says a lot about the strength of a person. The irony is that it takes the same degree of commitment to live a healthy lifestyle and be healthy as it does to choose *not* to live a healthy lifestyle and be unhealthy. Ultimately, the more enjoyment you get out of doing something, the more you're encouraged to do it again but if it's a chore then that's the emotional connection you will have with anything that resists you along your path.

Why am I *now* committed to making the necessary changes in my life?

....

....

What will my life look like 20 years from now if I continue living the way I do?

....

....

Motivation

Are you looking for a short-term or a long-term solution? As already mentioned, this book isn't for those looking to lose weight within a set period of time, it's for the realistic person who is fed up of living a life restricted by the way they look and has feelings of unhappiness.

Your motivation for losing weight is key to your success, so let's revisit the above questions and look again at answering them with complete honesty.

Why should you make the changes within your life?

....

....

What happens if you fail to change your eating habits?

....

....

How will your life improve by eating nutritionally rich foods?

....

....

What will you do with your improved and increased energy?

....

....

What positive aspects of this change will be reflected in your loved ones?

....

....

Why is now the right time to make these massive changes?

....

....

Do you deserve to be fit, healthy and happy?

....

....

Why will you never go back to being the way you were?

....

....

"Life is 10% what happens to me and 90% how I react to it." – Charles Swindoll

Skinny-Fat and Fat-Fat, DON'T Be Fooled

Okay, fat reality check time. We now know what fat is on a nutritional level but it's time to consider what it is in relation to the size of a person. There are many factors to be considered here. For example, someone who is six feet tall and weighs 13 stone is going to look very different to someone who weighs the same but is only five feet tall. Weight and fat are two completely different aspects of size yet weight seems to be considered the overall deciding factor by most when it comes to health.

The common assumption is that a heavy person must be a fat person but there's more to fat than just weight.

Skinny-fat – this describes the person who rarely eats, fails to exercise, and generally speaking will be a smoker in a stressful job (often in sales or accounting) with a dependant family at home. They are skinny but they hold more body fat than muscle, and the lack of quality nutrition actually causes a lack of growth and therefore skinniness. They are effectively functioning on the minimum levels of nutritional value, generally sourced through a diet of foods low in protein and carbohydrate and high in saturated fats.

Fat-fat – this describes the person who consumes too much and does too little in terms of physical exercise. Generally speaking, they adopt a lazy attitude to most things in life, other than things of immediate interest and this leads to a failure to recognise the importance of nutrition and its effect on their overall health and wellbeing. In most cases, a fat-fat person will stick to the minimum nutritional guidelines set out by the government and they will often use 'genetics' as a reason for being the way they are.

I feel it's important to mention this now because people often arrive at my seminars with preconceived ideas concerning size. The ultimate aim is to shift your focus away from skinny versus fat to see a fat-neutral state as the way forward in terms of health as well as self-perception. We need fat to live and we also need muscle so aiming to sit nicely between skinny and fat is the way to begin enjoying being in your body.

How much fat would I be happy with on my body?

....

....

How much fat is too much?

....

....

How can I achieve a fat-neutral self-perception?

....

....

Why Do You Want to Lose Weight – Please Be Honest!

Vanity – if you are looking to lose weight simply for vanity reasons, then here is the shocker: Over 90% of my clients who lie when they answer the question of *why* end up back where they started. They have a goal, they lose weight – they then flip back to old habits and put the weight back on. Losing weight to change the way you look is a big motivator but it's important not to let it be the main reason. It's a big temptation, but by focusing on the way you look you run the risk of achieving your ideal look, being happy with it, and then forgetting everything you've learned on your journey to get there.

Trying to fit in – another temptation to avoid is making changes to your diet simply to fit in with the current trend. This is increasingly popular in modern culture as social media helps to spread the word on the latest celebrity endorsed new (which really just means re-branded) diet. The moment an airbrushed celebrity shares "the secret" of their instant and fabulous new look, people are very quick to jump on the bandwagon – believing the same instant results will be theirs.

Trending diets have been around for the last 80 years and the number of 'new' diets appears to be increasing daily. Of course, we can't deny the evolution of medicine and science and the fact that we're still learning new concepts, but let's just think about the last 20 years or so and make some clear observations:

•   Obesity rates are climbing daily

•   It is reported that obesity and related illnesses will bankrupt the NHS by 2022

•   Fast food is becoming a staple in the majority of daily diets

•   Jobs involving physical labour are decreasing as the use of technology is increasing

•   The population is increasing and living space is decreasing

•   Home economics is no longer taught in most schools

•   Children are no longer participating in daily sports or outdoor activities.

•   Expectations to perform at higher levels for extended times.

These are just a few observations but when looked at collectively, the reason why we have these issues stands out. Avoid the temptation to follow a trend; the information contained within this book is a cut back and functional solution to get your diet back on track and achieve the results you want – no frills, just simple and honest advice.

To please another – this is a tricky subject that comes up frequently during my boot-camps. Changing the way you look to please another isn't going to deliver the results you think it will. The change has to come from within you and for your own reasons, not the reasons of another.

"Your time is limited; so don't waste it living someone else's life." – Steve Jobs

If you're having relationship issues because of a partner's behaviour and attitude to your weight, then avoid the belief that losing weight will change those behaviours. Losing weight *will* change your behaviour as you gain greater self-confidence but you must also address the reaction from your partner – has anything really changed? This is a subject that could fill a book of its own so, for now, take my advice and change because **you** want to, not because someone else tells you to.

Task: Grab a pen and write down five top reasons why you should lose weight. Mix up the answers with both long and short-term objectives. Keep the language used positive and avoid the temptation to over exaggerate.

....

....

....

....

....

....

Exercise

As already mentioned, and in simplistic terms, energy that isn't used will be stored as fat. The human body is designed to move but with modern living no longer requiring the same degree of physical effort and daily tasks no longer as labour intensive as they once were, we need to make a conscious effort to introduce movement into our lives.

For those who don't currently partake in it, exercise is generally thought of as something that induces aches and pains and requires hours of sweating over something each week. Exercise is seen as a chore but in truth it can be so much more. The act of movement can be anything from a daily walk to work, to circuits/classes, to dancing or tennis, or any other activity at all that gets you moving.

A lack of exercise causes endless issues on both a physical and mental level. Movement aids digestion and helps to cleanse the body as well as generating the release of essential mood enhancing chemicals that simulate positive thinking and performance.

What can you implement right now that will increase the movement within your life?

....

....

How much time can you commit every day to additional movement?

....

....

What You Should Be Doing

There are many different types of exercise programmes on the market, all with unique benefits and designed to suit a variety of fitness levels. Having worked with many hundreds of people, I have altered and adapted my programmes to engage each aspect of the body while increasing the cardiovascular capacity.

I've included two of the most popular programmes below and you can use them as often as you wish. However, the people who report the best results tend to take part in some form of activity at least three times a week, gradually increasing to five. At the back of the book I've included an explanation of each of the exercises, but they can also be found online.

Added note: there is no substitute to training as part of a group. Being in the company of others very often boosts motivation, increasing the ability of all concerned, and it provides accountability. However, I do appreciate that not everyone has the opportunity or the resources to attend a club or gym.

When completing the exercises below, the aim is to raise your breathing rate to the point that you can just about hold a conversation, but your sentences are becoming shorter! Make sure you have enough room around you and only start when it's safe to do so.

Metabolic Fat Burning Workout # 1

Warm Up – 1 Minute of Running on the Spot

Lunges Alternate	24 Reps
Squats	24 Reps
Lunge to Rotation	24 Reps
Squat Jumps	12 Reps
Hold the Plank	30 seconds

30 Second Rest

Press Ups Narrow Rest	50 Seconds Exercise, 10 Seconds
Press Ups Normal Rest	50 Seconds Exercise, 10 Seconds
Press Ups Staggered Rest	50 Seconds Exercise, 10 Seconds
Press Ups Hands Out Rest	50 Seconds Exercise, 10 Seconds
Bent Over Rows Rest	50 Seconds Exercise, 10 Seconds
Shoulder press Rest	50 Seconds Exercise, 10 Seconds
Upright Row/ Lateral Raise Rest	50 Seconds Exercise, 10 Seconds
Bicep Curls Rest	50 Seconds Exercise, 10 Seconds
Triceps Extensions Rest	50 Seconds Exercise, 10 Seconds

Sprint on the Spot – 20 seconds on 20 seconds off 20 seconds on. Rest 20 seconds then repeat twice.

Crawl Outs Rest	30 Seconds Exercise, 15 Seconds
Burpees Rest	30 Seconds Exercise, 30 Seconds

High Knees – 20 seconds on 20 seconds off 20 seconds on. Rest 20 seconds then repeat twice.

Crunches	50 Seconds Exercise, 10 Seconds Rest
Obliques	50 Seconds Exercise, 10 Seconds Rest
Reverse Curls	50 Seconds Exercise, 10 Seconds Rest
Cross Overs	50 Seconds Exercise, 10 Seconds Rest
Bicycle	50 Seconds Exercise, 10 Seconds Rest
Kick Outs	16, 12, 8, 4, 2 slow, 1 hold for 10 seconds,
10 fast (each side)	
Plank to Press Up	50 Seconds Exercise, 10 Seconds Rest
Side Plank	50 Seconds Exercise, 10 Seconds Rest
Squat Thrusts	50 Seconds Exercise, 10 Seconds Rest

Metabolic Fat Burning Workout # 2

Warm Up – 1 Minute of Running on the Spot

30 Second Rest

Lunges Alternate	24 Reps
Squats	24 Reps
Lunge to Rotation	24 Reps
Squat Jumps	12 Reps
Hold the Plank	30 Seconds

30 Second Rest

Ladders – 3 Exercises in Each Ladder Drill 1-10 Reps of Each Then Back Down From 10-1

Bent Over Rows
Shoulder Press
Bicep Curls

1-10 Reps of Each Then Back Down From 10-1

Press Ups
Squats – holding weight between legs
Triceps Extensions

1-10 Reps of Each Then Back Down From 10-1

Squats
Burpees
Crunches

1-10 Reps of Each Then Back Down From 10-1

Obliques (each side)
Reverse Curls
Hip Raises

Cardio Circuit

Sprint on the Spot	50 Seconds Exercise, 10 Seconds Rest
High Knees	50 Seconds Exercise, 10 Seconds Rest
Heel Flicks	50 Seconds Exercise, 10 Seconds Rest
Crawl Outs	50 Seconds Exercise, 10 Seconds Rest
Side Jumps	50 Seconds Exercise, 10 Seconds Rest

When can you commit to one of the above?

Day......................Time........................

Why is now the right time to set this?

....

....

How are you going to ensure that nothing interrupts this time?

....

....

The Stages of Transition

There are 3 stages that you must go through in order for you to reach your goal long term.

The first stage is the Weight Loss stage, the second stage is the

Transformation stage and the third stage is the Maintenance stage.

I'm going to use somebody who would like to lose 3 stone as an example to explain the principle behind the stages of transition. So let's say that this person is starting off at 13 stone and they want to get down to 10 stone. In order for them to go from where they are now to their goal weight, we know that it is going to take a certain amount of time and in my experience typically this will take most people around 6 months.

In order for them to lose the 3 stone, we know that for them to get to 10 stone they will need to make certain changes.

Would you agree that your body right now is a direct reflection of what you do daily?

The first thing we need to change is our nutrition, we need to implement the 40/30/30 rule and we need to look at hydration, the ideal amount of water you should drink on a daily basis is 1 litre per 50lbs that you weigh, so if you weigh 200lbs (14 stone) then you will need to drink 4 Litres of water per day.

How much water should you be drinking per day?

....

The second thing we need to look at is the exercise and you should be exercising for a minimum of 2-3 sessions per week. 1 session per week will not cut it, you will need to start to get your body moving regularly and start to get lots of mobility through your muscles and joints.

The last thing is your behaviours, so behaviour change is vital; it's the psychology behind all of this stuff. In the most basic of terms it's down to something called your subconscious and conscious mind. 98% of what you do and what you have in your life right now is based on your subconscious mind, it's the thing that makes your heart beat 100,000 times per day it's the thing that when you get up in the morning have a shower get ready for work, eat breakfast and drive or walk to work and do your job. Most of these activities are done on autopilot, you no longer have to think about the processes of doing this stuff you just do it naturally, that's your subconscious mind controlling that.

2% of what you do on a daily basis is conscious, things you remember to do. Like if you have an appointment somewhere, which is outside your ordinary pattern, you will have to write it down on your calendar and remind yourself and start to think about where you are going.

Now when most people try and lose weight they try and do it consciously, they say things like "starting from Monday I'm going to start to diet and cut out the biscuits, crisps, chocolate, wine, takeaways and start to take the stairs at work instead of the lift". (Now I'm going to be really generous and call it Friday but normally it's a Wednesday) By Friday then, most people normally turn round to their partners or family and friends and say I've been so good this week I deserve a little treat, that Friday night treat rolls into Saturday then into Sunday and then into Monday. On Monday we have this internal battle with ourselves where we say I have already ruined this week I'm going to start again next Monday.

It's called the next Monday syndrome and I'm sure you have gone through that before.

The key thing in order for you to get from where you are now, down to where you want to go is to put yourself in the frame of mind, as though you have already achieved your goal and what I mean by that is not sitting there wishful thinking saying "I wish I was 10 stone, I wish I was 10 stone." You've got to do the things you would be doing at your goal weight and if you were sitting here reading this book at your goal weight, guess what you would be doing?

Eating 40/30/30, hydrating your body, exercising regularly and consciously thinking about doing this stuff as apposed to what you are doing now.

When most people get down to their goal weight, what do they do?

Well most people who reach their goal stop and put all of the weight back on.

How many times have you done this?

This is called yo yo dieting and yo yo dieting is a psychological thing, which a lot of people don't really understand, here is how it works;

Imagine that your subconscious, conscious mind and your body is where you are now, we are going to put our conscious mind where we want to get to and start to do the things necessary to get to our goal and therefore our body will also reach our goal weight. Once our conscious mind and body is at our goal weight, most people think they have achieved their goal, they flip back to subconscious or autopilot which is still at their original weight, therefore their body realigns with their original weight and that's why most people yo yo diet.

The key thing to long term fat loss, which is what all of you want is; for how ever long it takes you to lose the weight you want to lose, you must do the same thing for the same amount of time to change your subconscious behaviours. The longer you are at your goal weight the longer it changes your subconscious behaviours to be in line with your conscious mind and body. So if you stop halfway your body will realign with the subconscious mind. The key thing is to follow it all the way through to the end until your subconscious is in line with your conscious mind and body. That's when you have achieved your goal because that's when your subconscious mind acts and behaves at your goal weight. This is when I say to my clients during the maintenance stage you must make it part of your lifestyle, you must start to make this all be part of the person you want to be and the person you might want to be is full of energy, full of confidence, can wear whichever clothes that you want to wear. For this to happen you must make exercise and eating healthy part of your new identity and that's how long term Health is created.

Top Tip: Cold Showers Ideal For Sleep And Fat Loss

I know you are probably thinking that you could never have a cold shower, here is why you should: Cold showers help balance your adrenal glands and lower cortisol (master stress hormone responsible for belly fat) so the cold shower will not only help you sleep but also it will help you reduce belly fat. Sleep is vital in the recovery process; it's when your body repairs itself.

This is what I advise to my members, have a cold shower for 5 minutes at 10:30pm then go straight to bed.

Chapter Five

"No nonsense advice and motivation to get you guaranteed results. If you are ready for the effort, Dan is ready to guide you in your journey with his wealth of experience and knowledge. Highly recommend." Carol A.

Food – More Than Just Food

Just remember the old adage, *"You are what you eat,"* and you won't go far wrong.

Consuming quality food becomes even more essential, if not critically so, when you are ill or struggling with chronic feelings of being under the weather. Becoming better at something means taking steps to learn how to improve and therefore do better in that something, right? Learning how to feel better through learning how to eat better is no different. The better your understanding of food and its effects on your body – both emotionally and physically – the stronger a position you put yourself in to be able to take control and improve your mental and physical health.

Think about this for a moment:

On a recent trip to a hospital, I was amazed by the types of foods being served in the canteens there, and not only that, but by the physical condition of those treating the ill. I estimate that an average of 80% of all the staff/medical professionals I witnessed were clinically obese (I consider someone to be obese if their knees rub together when they walk.) Surely this doesn't make sense. We go to hospital to be treated because we are ill but while we're there we're fed rubbish – bland, colourless food – and we're treated by a number of professionals who apparently fail to take any notice of *their* industry recommendations.

Take a look at this NHS (National Health Service) report:

Being obese increases your risk of developing a number of serious and potentially life-threatening diseases, such as:

- Type 2 diabetes
- Heart disease
- Some types of cancer, such as breast cancer and colon cancer
- Stroke

In addition, obesity can damage your quality of life and can often trigger depression.

Source: http://www.nhs.uk

In my opinion, the above simply highlights the need for re-education in terms of the practical application of being able to eat, live and succeed, in the most vibrant and healthiest way possible.

Feed your life with HARD facts, not myths … let's get real!

If you've reached this far in the book, the likelihood is that you have *really* identified that you need to change something... perhaps the pain has become unbearable, or perhaps you've simply identified that things can no longer continue as they are. Either way, movement is always good.

However, beware of self-affirmations during your dietary journey.

Self-affirmations will either envelope you in a visualised reality or disassociate you from the truth. With food, it's usually the latter. When you disassociate yourself from the truth, you say things to yourself such as, "It doesn't matter," or "Things will get better." You might also make strong, bold statements such as, "I will change in the New Year" or, "Just as soon as such and such has happened I'll change …"

Of course, putting your head in the sand in such a way will almost always create a situation in which you inevitably become someone you could have avoided had you known the problems that would arise from these affirmations.

Ask yourself this: isn't it time you started living the life you always wanted?

Use affirmations, but ensure that they linguistically benefit you. The affirmations you use should move eating away from something that's a chore to something that's exciting. You control your life; it knows no boundaries other than those you give it. Allow it to run away with you and that's what will happen, but grasp it hard, control it and allow it to become something special… and it will.

What affirmation would inspire you to keep moving forward?

....

....

What additional education do you require in order to feel fully confident with your new journey?

....

....

Set yourself new goals based around what you have learnt thus far. Create a picture of a connection between food and a life boosting transformation beyond your wildest dreams, and avoid looking at food as something, which has brought about negative emotions in the past.

The Foods You Eat Vs. The Lifestyle You Live

Many times I talk with people who have been on any number of courses and training programmes or attended countless lectures and I'll always ask them to tell me in what way they've applied what they've learnt to their own lives. In over 70% of cases, they never have. They've gone on all of those courses yet they've failed to take action on anything they've learned. **Knowing** stuff is not enough, it's only by **applying** what you know that you can make change happen. Apply everything you have learnt so far and I can GUARANTEE that you will notice complete change in all aspects of your life.

"The world needs dreamers and the world needs doers. But above all, the world needs dreamers who do" – Sarah Ban Breathnach

Only follow those who are practising what they preach. Something I have noticed A LOT within the FF industry (food and fitness industry) is that there are a great amount of people who tell but they don't apply: they talk the talk but they don't walk the walk. Only seek advice from those who have taken action to achieve what you want to achieve and therefore look like they actually believe in what they say.

It's my experience there are a great number of fitness instructors and dieticians who don't look like they're taking their own advice. For this reason, whenever I'm looking for a mentor in some new adventure, I always look for a person who not only looks like they are doing as they say but also doing what they passionately believe in. I believe in my fitness programme and I'm constantly working towards improving it by making small adjustments along the way. Sometimes I learn through experience that there's a better way and I adjust my programme accordingly, and other times I learn that something is no longer effective and therefore I discard it. Either way, I'm constantly learning and I take what I learn forwards with me to ensure I continue to achieve the best results possible.

Stagnant programmes or thinking patterns will not evolve, and there are plenty of people out there selling products or programmes that are years out of date. Someone who truly believes in their message or product will be constantly moving and looking for ways to make improvements because they are 100% committed to delivering something of value – something that is constantly evolving. What I'm saying is that no matter what you're being told, make sure you're being told by someone who lives and breathes what he or she says and is highly committed to making themselves a better and stronger person. When you know that someone else has done it, you gain the motivation and confidence to do it for yourself, hence the reason why I would always where possible join a group or bootcamp to gain additional motivation, accountability and someone with the knowledge to guide you.

Where can you go that will support and help you where needed?

....

....

Who would you consider to be a suitable role model?

....

....

Reality Check

Okay, now is as good a time as any to pause, take a breath and take a reality check. Throughout our lives, most of us accept that what is seen on the outside is predetermined by what is on the inside; we accept that who we are on the inside is reflected in the way we appear on the outside. So, how about flipping it? When working with clients in my practice, I ask them to consider and describe what the person on the inside is saying to person on the outside … and vice-versa.

In the majority of cases, the person on the inside will blame a number of emotions and past beliefs or experiences for the way they feel and the way they have acted as a result, meaning the way they have allowed themselves to form an unhealthy relationship with food. When we flip it and ask the person on the outside to describe the person on the inside, the focus more often than not switches away from the emotions and is placed on the physical and very *real* aspects of their life.

What we then have is two conflicting accounts of the 'truth'. A reality check is therefore essential and we have to break it down to discover the REAL TRUTH.

This process isn't solely focused on an individual's weight, but on their appearance, logic and overall health. The reality check helps to uncover the language each individual is using to describe themselves and the identity this gives them based on their overall appearance.

In other words, if you have become an unhealthy slob who consumes ready meals and gallons of fizzy drinks then that's the appearance you will put out to the rest of the world – both the outer you and the inner you will reflect this identity. You can't lie about obesity or poor skin/health and the inner emotions you are experiencing will reveal the same truth.

How has the outside world seen you in the past?

....

....

What changes have you made so they don't see you like this in the future?

....

....

Why are you motivated to make these changes in your life right now?

....

....

So how will these changes appear when you improve your diet? The first change will be an internal change. It's likely that you'll go through a period of unrest initially until the clock is reset, but you'll then begin to feel the benefits of extended energy. You'll start to sleep better and as a result your complexion will change, and this leads into starting to feel more confident about your appearance. As this change happens, the language you use to describe yourself will also change and this is where the biggest impact occurs. By simply changing your diet, you change outwardly *and* inwardly and these changes provide the motivation to make larger lifestyle changes happens.

Now, there is a slight caveat: some people have reached a point of giving up internally and when this is the case they no longer care about their external appearance. They adopt an attitude of, "That's just the way I am," but this is tragic in my view. It is one thing to be accepting of your fate but it's quite another to limit your potential in life by resisting change and stubbornly refusing to adapt to doing things differently.

"I attribute my success to this: I never gave or took any excuse." – Florence Nightingale

What can I do to ensure that I will not give up?

....

....

Moving forward, the life you live is only as good as you make it, right? Well, yes and no. It's certainly true that if you want to change your life then you're going to have to take action to make those changes happen. But, as you become open to making changes, you will find there are plenty of people out there who are willing to offer their advice on just what changes you should make and many of your nearest and dearest will suddenly become diet and nutrition experts, all too willing to add their opinion to the mix. Change for the sake of change is not necessarily a good thing. Following the advice of 'experts' who clearly don't follow their own advice is unlikely to bring you the changes you want. You'll hear all sorts of things and that's fine, but you need to know the exact direction you want to go in and the purpose of *your* adventure. When you're clear about the changes you want to see happen in your life, you're then in a position to discard any comments that are not relevant to you and the changes you want to achieve. Trust me, as soon as other people notice the positive changes in your complexion and they see that you're full of energy, they'll be asking *you* for your secrets and expert advice.

Building A Solid Support Team

As With Any Worthwhile Endeavour We All Need Support.....

During this program you will be stepping outside your comfort zone as you change your eating and lifestyle habits. You may find it challenging at some points as you make these changes and transform your body shape and there may be times when you feel like venturing off the nutrition plan.

This is when you need your allies around you for support. These may be your co-workers, friends, family and loved ones?

Identify & Use Your Allies

So who could be your allies?

....

....

Who are the people in your life that you know you can count on to be there for you when you need it? ...No matter what!

Speak with these people and let them know what you are doing and that you would like their support over the next month as you make these changes.

So who could be your allies?

Task: Write your allies down:

....

....

....

Identify Your Saboteurs

What about those that do not give you the support you need to succeed?

Just as there will be people who want to support you to do well, there will also be people who do the opposite, who will undermine what you are doing.

When you've identified your potential saboteurs, there is no need to say anything to them.

Simply, be aware of them and be conscious of how they will help or hinder you.

Why might people try to sabotage your success?

There are a number of reasons why someone might do this. It doesn't mean they are bad, their reasons may be because they care.

Here's a few guesses as to why some people will do it:

- Maybe they don't want or are scared of you succeeding,

- Maybe they want to make themselves feel better,
- Maybe they want to save you from making a mistake,
- Maybe they want to protect you from disappointment,
- or Suddenly they are an "Expert" on the subject!
- Who knows the reason! Just realise, they're going to show up!

So who might your saboteurs be?

Task: Write down your possible saboteurs * *Might be an idea not to let them see this page ;-)*

....

....

....

Tomorrow Is A Better Day ...

You are bound to experience a mass number of obstacles when changing anything. For me, the main obstacle was having lived a certain way for nearly 30 years and therefore having well-established habitual eating patterns. However, with each day of your new eating pattern, you begin to establish new habits and your old habits are soon left behind. I have met and worked with many people who have made this transition into healthy eating and as a result have transformed the way they act and live into a lifestyle that would previously only have been associated with someone many years their junior.

Nutrition, if you haven't guessed it already, is more than just the produce you put into your mouth, it's a whole new you; it's a whole new way of living and it's something you can use to better your life and extend your life. With this in mind, isn't it time you took back control of your life?

Ask yourself this: if you discovered you had cancer or diabetes and that your life was limited unless you made some changes right now this very moment, how long would you have to think about it before you committed to making those changes?

....

....

For most people, a switch to nutritionally good food can change their life around completely. As humans, we are fortunate to have the option of choice; the choice to do something or not, and in my world, that choice is just as important as the outcome. Out of all of the people I've worked with and helped to change all three pillars – lifestyle, nutrition and fitness – not one has ever asked me to help them change back to the person they were before. Why? Because we have choice, it's just that we tend to take our health for granted until it is too late.

Why wait for the change to happen? You have the ability to live a life as good as the healthiest person you know or as bad as the unhealthiest person you know, the deciding factor is nothing more than your choice. Only you can decide what you consume: factors such as money and geographic location can influence choices but they are rarely a valid reason for continuing to make poor choices.

"It is not necessary to change. Survival is not mandatory" – W. Edwards
Deming

What Do You Value?

When asked to consider your response to being told you were suffering a terminal illness, it's my hope that this triggered some deeper realisations in terms of the actual value you place on your own life.

Through food, I have changed my value on life. Seeing through my own eyes how food and nutrition affects thinking as well as the physical body has been enough to ensure that I never, EVER, go back to the way I was. My value is knowing that I can always be better; just because something didn't work in the past does not mean that it won't in the future, and that through consuming the right things I allow my body to work in the best possible form, thereby protecting me, supporting me, and allowing me to live the life I deserve.

Why do you want your body to work in the best way possible?

....

....

What are you looking forward to doing with your new body?

....

....

Perhaps you're wondering how I can be so certain that I will never go back. Well, I'm certain because I've been around people grasping onto life; people who failed to take the action needed until it was too late; people who chose to abuse their bodies for years, and people who were consciously aware of doing wrong but only took heed of the damage being done once it had become too late. There are millions of people around the world suffering because of obesity and other dietary related illnesses and one thing is guaranteed; each one of them would turn back the clock and make a change if it meant they were able to spend just a few more days with loved ones, or perhaps be at a special event they will now miss.

The only time something becomes too late is when you fail to take the action when it comes into your mind for the first time. I call these the 'late lates' – a string of 'too lates' that then turn into "later". Be aware of falling into this mind-set. Putting things off for another time can be a slippery slope, especially if changing your diet is something you've thought about before but failed to take action on.

"Life is what happens to you while you're busy making other plans." – John Lennon

Remember, it doesn't matter what your motivations or reasons are, the most important thing is that you are doing it because you are fully aware of the health benefits associated with being healthy and the massive improvements it will bring to your lifestyle.

It's never too late… simple!

Remember the Art of Replacement

Have you ever been in a situation where you have given something up and all you can do is think about it? No matter what you do to distract yourself, the one thing you can't have is the one thing you want, right?

Smokers and dieters are among those who are most likely to experience this. Cigarettes and food are the only things they can think about as soon as they try to give them up. The reason for this is the relationship and close connection they have with these items. The things that attracted them into the relationship in the first place become the things they focus on when they can no longer have them, and the things they find themselves 'craving' and wanting back.

To rid yourself of these cravings and feelings of want you need to understand the art of replacement. Simply taking something away isn't going to work as this leaves a hole that needs to be filled – hence the craving. Replacing the something that is taken away with something else fills the hole and curbs the craving, but the replacement must of course be a genuinely healthy option. Getting into the habit of doing without can be tough and it's for this reason that the art of replacement is likely to be much more effective in the long term as a new and positive habit is formed.

Have you ever tried to take an ice cream away from a baby, or a bone from a dog?

The subconscious mind is very clever at identifying things that are missing; the conscious skill is the art of replacing it until the new replacement is viewed as the better alternative.

What challenges in the past can be replaced with something more positive in the future?

....

....

Isn't It Time You Started Listening to Your Body?

There are many reasons why you may already have started to change the way you eat and just as many for wanting to be able to change if you haven't started already. Each reason is unique to you and each is a valued reason I am sure, but one thing many of us within western culture have forgotten to do is to listen to our body.

We should all learn how to listen to our bodies and we should all then take the time to actually do it. Your body is really good at describing exactly what it needs. For example, think about the way you feel when you're thirsty ... your body lets you know it needs hydration. What about when you're hungry? Once again, your body lets you know it needs fuel; but what about when you're full? This question is not quite so straightforward to answer. The majority of us know when we're full so our bodies *do* let us know, the problem is that the majority of us fail to listen ... we continue to eat even though our bodies have signalled that we're full. We overeat because we choose to over-rule the signals that we're full in favour of continuing to gorge on the foods we mistakenly believe are making us feel good.

The human body has evolved to survive but unfortunately many of the people I meet are barely doing that. Through a general lack of understanding about nutrition, the diet many people 'survive' on today no longer fits into our evolutionary needs and the end result is obesity and the associated poor health issues. As a species we've become lazy, not only in our tendency to avoid exercise but also in our attitude to eating and our food choices.

"Life isn't about getting and having, it's about giving and being." – Kevin Kruse

Important recap: you have absolute control over your journey in life. If you want to be sad, unhealthy and end up reducing your life by 10 or even more years then carry on. But, if you want to grasp life by the balls and make the most of every day, then you NEED to focus on re-educating yourself and gaining an understanding of nutrition and food. Change the focus away from what you can't have and what you can't do and place it on what you can have and what you can do. This change in thinking goes a long way towards improving the way in which you view food and this, in turn, gives you the ability to overcome any cravings you may have.

Negative people generally mix with negative people – it's called bonding through moaning – don't be one of them.

Top Tip: avoid where possible beating yourself up over eating a certain way in the past. You are now on the mend and taking steps to change your life for the better. Remember, it's not magic, it's just good eating. Commit to eating healthily at least 80% of the time and accept that the occasional chocolate bar (or similar) will not do that much harm.

You'll quickly notice that the more your body undergoes the transformation – releasing and letting go of those unwanted chemicals – you'll start to crave healthier, more beneficial ingredients in your daily diet. In fact, you'll very quickly notice that the majority of foods you once thought were packed full of flavour will become quite foul!

Get excited about the positive things this journey will bring as it's essential that you keep a positive mind-set. The way you look at your nutrition and think about food has more of an effect than you may have realised. Positive thinking will now become more important than ever before and this includes loving your body from the outset. Starting to love and respect your body will in turn manifest into becoming a stronger person. Think about it this way; the more you love yourself, the more respect you will have for yourself, and the more you will consciously think about the foods you consume as a result.

You Only Live Twice

This title plays a significant role in my past and I'm certain it's one that many others can relate to. Within our lives, we can live one life with one diet and accept one path or we can grasp the opportunity to change it and live a second life. What we consume affects everything; how we act and feel changes the way we see the outside world. The changes in our diet can affect everything in our life – 55% of the way we communicate may be via physiology but 80% of how we perform is the result of what we consume.

The importance of diet cannot be stressed enough. If you fail to look after the factor that controls the majority of how you function, you will never reach your full potential. Accept that you have the opportunity to live twice – the old you and now the new you. Your second life is going to be the lifestyle you choose to maintain for the rest of your life, and choosing to make changes in the foods you consume now will allow you to finally be the person you have already dreamed of becoming.

What is your life going to look like 10 years from now with your new changes?

....

....

What are you most excited about doing?

....

....

Time Vs. Benefits With Food Production

This is something I find highly frustrating, not solely because it's an excuse used by many people without thinking it through, but because it factually couldn't be any further than the truth. I can prepare a highly nutritional meal within half the amount of time it takes to microwave a meal and I can juice in half the time it takes to make a cup of coffee.

Time management may seem like a strange topic of discussion in relation to changing/ altering your diet, but if you are someone who is living a fast-paced lifestyle then you're going to need some kind of routine and forward planning in place. The solution to any perceived time restraints is to prepare your meals the night before and use plastic, sealable pots. It couldn't be any easier. Nuts, seeds, beans, vegetables and even juices can all be prepared in advance and stored ready for the next day. Grabbing a pre-prepared pot is a lot faster than driving through your local fast food drive-thru or queuing at your local supermarket, in fact, when you think about it, there is nothing fast about fast-food. The only thing it's fast for is speeding up diet related illnesses.

I've mentioned a few times that improving your diet will lead to improvements in your energy levels. This is not a myth, or something made up by 'fitties' to annoy 'fatties', it's a fact. Think about the logic behind it; vegetables and all things natural absorb energy from the outside world and use it for growth. We can then utilise it and transfer it into our bodies through digestion.

Use linguistics to look at food differently – start using words such as dirty, poor, nasty or disgusting to repel any positive connections with processed products.

Why is dedicating the right amount of time to a diet key in your future?

....

....

How much time are you committing to improving the quality of your life?

....

....

Why is this important?

....

....

How and where can you overcome any obstacles?

....

....

Challenges – How Are You Going to Get Over Them?

As with any form of change, you will meet a whole host of different challenges along the way. You'll be subjected to criticism, you'll doubt yourself, and you'll even start to wonder if it's all worth it. You'll perhaps come up with a number of reasons why your old way of life was better, but I can promise you that if you follow my advice with 100% commitment and focus, you'll be able to make positive changes to your diet that last a lifetime. You won't want to go back to your old ways and who knows, you'll perhaps start to make changes in other areas of your life.

Habits take time to change, but avoid the temptation to slip into a false sense of security. Be honest from the very beginning and you'll see results appear a lot faster than you would if you were to stay within the security of the unhappiness that you're experiencing at the moment.

It's all about tomorrow – so many people I know want to know the shortcut to losing those additional pounds in body fat or how to get a six-pack within two weeks. The only shortcut to any of these things is to take action today so that tomorrow will be a less of a challenge. We would all love to be able to change our diet overnight and wake up looking like an Adonis in the morning but it's not going to happen. Committing to making changes in your diet will get you 80% of the way towards being your 'best you' but the other two factors of lifestyle and fitness must be addressed in order to get you all the way there.

Getting the Family on the Healthy Eating Team

You'd think it would be easy to get partners and spouses on board but it has been my experience that family members can be the biggest cynics of them all. This is especially true if they have seen you 'try' something new in past only to have given up when things weren't quite going the way you hoped. I have no shame in admitting that I have been that person.

What I am getting at is that no matter how highly motivated you may be, there's no guarantee that those around you will share your passion. However, if you are a parent, you can share your enthusiasm with your children and positively influence their food choices. If you are changing your diet for the better then by default you should be changing your children's diet for the better.

I love food and share my experiences where I can; food is my daily celebration and reward.

Each New Year, it makes me laugh to see overweight adults out buying up every new slimming product on the market yet continuing to buy the same old junk foods for their children. Does it make sense to improve your own diet but feed those you love the most the foods that led to you being unhappy and buying up slimming products in desperation? No!

My recommendation is to start gently with children by introducing them to the fun aspects of food. You'll get a much better buy-in if they are having fun experimenting with new foods rather than being told it's something they must do. Keep your whole family healthy by only buying nutritionally rich food and keeping your kitchen cupboards free of any nutritionally poor options. An easy motto to go by is – *If it's not in the house then I can't eat it.*

Chapter Six

"After retiring from my second career, I was very unfit and pretty overweight, was bullied into Dan's fitness class by my wife and after the first session, swore I would never return. Now, 3 years of U.U. later, I am almost 2 stone lighter and fitter than I have been for a very long time. I have never been a lover of exercise and I can't say, hand on heart, that I run into every class with 'eager anticipation', but with Dans support and encouragement, as well as a very friendly group of people, it has become a part of my (hopefully extended) life. Thank you both." Steve H.

Recipes

Now that we've covered the thinking, values and purposes of food, you will hopefully have changed the way in which you view the basics of your dietary requirements. Over the next few pages I've included some recipes for really tasty and interesting dishes. There are plenty to give you variety but not so many that you become bewildered by choices. Each one is quick to prepare and nutritionally rich in protein, carbohydrates, fats and minerals. They are designed to kick-start a cleansing process, enabling you to start building a diet based on the food choices you are likely to consume in the future. Some of the ingredients may be new to you, perhaps even slightly alien, but all I ask is that you give them a try and then make adaptations to suit your palette.

Think for a moment; how many different types of meals do you consume on a weekly basis?

....

....

How often do you change your breakfast?

....

....

What can you do to overcome any mindful objections when making these meals?

....

....

What is the reason behind changing your diet?

....

....

5 Healthy Breakfasts

Healthy Breakfast Number 1

Scrambled Eggs with Smoked Salmon (Serves 2)

Ingredients

- 4 large eggs
- 3 tablespoons milk
- 125g smoked salmon
- 10g butter

Directions:

1. Melt the butter into a frying pan over a low heat
2. Break the eggs into a bowl and beat them with a fork seasoning with salt and pepper.
3. When the butter has melted pour in the eggs and increase the heat slightly.
4. When it starts to thicken add the salmon and the milk and stir in well, keep stirring until all the liquid has nearly gone and then remove from the heat
5. Keep stirring until the scrambled egg is to the consistency you like
6. Serve with 2 ryvita biscuits of your choice

Healthy Breakfast Number 2

Natural Yoghurt, Almonds and Grapes

Ingredients

- 150g Natural yoghurt)
- 15g Whole almonds
- 6 Grapes, seedless

Directions:

1. Chop the grapes and almonds
2. add to the yoghurt to eat

Healthy Breakfast Number 3

Texas Eggs (Serves 2)

Ingredients

- 6 medium-large tomatoes or a large punnet of cherry tomatoes
- 1 red pepper, seeds removed chopped
- 1 onion, quartered (skin off)
- 3 peeled garlic cloves
- pinch of chilli powder, to taste
- 1 lemon
- 3-4 eggs
- Handful fresh basil leaves

Directions:

1. Preheat oven to gas mark 4
2. Heat an oven proof frying pan, add tomatoes, pepper, onion and garlic, dry fry for 10-15 mins until all the veg is softened.
3. Blitz or roughly chop, place back in pan add seasoning, chilli powder to taste. Add a little olive oil and lemon juice to freshen.
4. Create a well for each egg – crack them in. (max 4)
5. Place pan in oven for 5 mins until eggs are cooked (yolk still runny) sprinkle basil leaves over the top and serve.

Healthy Breakfast Number 4

Waldorf Smoothie

Ingredients

- 2 Apples
- 2 Celery Stalks
- 1 tbsp Tahini
- 100ml Live Bio Yoghurt
- 1 tsp Honey (optional)

Directions:

1. Juice your apples and celery – blend with tahini and yoghurt
2. Try and add more tahini/yoghurt to taste.
3. Whizz in a trickle of honey if you like.

Healthy Breakfast Number 5

Poached egg and mushrooms with Argentinian sauce (serves 2)

Ingredients

- 10g flat lead parsley
- 10g oregano
- Pinch of chilli flakes
- 2 tbsp apple cider vinegar
- 600g chestnut mushrooms
- Splash of olive oil
- 2 eggs
- 100g Baby leaf salad

Directions:

1. Finely chop or blitz parsley and oregano – place in a bowl and add pinch of chilli flakes, vinegar, and season – taste and adjust as required.
2. Clean and chop mushrooms into 1/4s. Warm olive oil in a pan, fry off the mushrooms, season and cook until golden brown.
3. Poach the eggs while the mushrooms are cooking. (Fill pan with hot kettle water, bring to the boil, turn heat down to a simmer, swirl water, crack eggs into a cup and slide into the pan)
4. Let them simmer for 3-5 mins (depending on how you like the yolks)
5. Rinse and dry the salad leaves, divide between two plates and serve eggs on tops, with a few spoonful's of sauce drizzled over the eggs.

5 Healthy Lunches

Healthy Lunch Number 1

Sweetcorn and Tuna Salad - (The mixed salad element serves 2, or can be used as an accompaniment for a dinner)

Ingredients

- Olive oil
- 1 small tin of sweetcorn
- 1 tin of Tuna
- Handful of Salad leaves
- 4 or 5 cherry tomatoes
- 2 tbsp Cottage Cheese
- 2 Rice Cakes/Ryvita
- 1 Lemon

Directions:

1. Drain your tuna and sweetcorn and empty into a bowl.
2. Chop your salad leaves, chop your tomatoes into ¼'s. Empty in with the tuna/sweetcorn. Season well and add a splash of olive oil and a squeeze of lemon juice. You can also grate a little zest into the bowl if you like.
3. Then spread your cottage cheese onto a rice cake and enjoy!

Healthy Lunch Number 2

Mediterranean Style Soup (serves 2)

Ingredients

1 punnet cherry plum tomatoes
1 fennel bulb
2 small red onions
1 red pepper
2 cloves garlic
1 sprig rosemary
A handful or fresh basil

Directions:

1. Preheat your oven to 200 degs C. Place a roasting try on the top shelf.
2. Put your tomatoes in a bowl, chop the feathery fronds off your fennel, chop into 3cm chunks. Halve the red pepper, scoop out the seeds and cut into chunks. Peel and chop your red onions into 1cm thick slices. Add all the veg to the tomatoes, season, gloss with olive oil and put all in your roasting tin. Cook for 20 mins in the oven.
3. After 20 mins, chop the rosemary and sprinkle over the veg and pop the garlic cloves in amongst the veg then put it back in the oven.
4. After 10 minutes remove from oven, squeeze the garlic cloves out of the skin. Add everything to a blender and blitz, adding up to 400-450 ml of boiling water, to bring to the desired soup consistency. Chop the basil and sprinkle over soup, as a garnish.

Healthy Lunch Number 3

Winter Pho with Seafood (serves 2)

Ingredients

2 leeks
1 carrot
1 red chilli
1 thumb of ginger
Bunch of watercress
3 garlic cloves
2 star anise
1 tbsp. of Lime juice and grated zest
1 punnet of chestnut mushrooms
10-12 peeled cooked prawns (you could substitute the prawns for leftover chicken breast strips, or other seafood.

Directions:

1. Cut your leeks into 4cm chunks, discard the dark green bits. Then finally chop lengthways. Rinse and drain.
2. Peel, scrub and julienne/finely slice the carrots. Peel and grate the ginger and garlic. Finely slice about a ¼ of the chilli, discard seeds.
3. Get a large saucepan hot, add the leek, carrot, chilli, ginger, garlic and star anise. Pour in 500ml of boiling water. Bring to the boil, lower heat and simmer for around 10 mins.
4. Then add the zest and lime juice.
5. Fry off the mushrooms separately and then add them to the pot along with the prawns, continue to simmer for around 10 minutes. Season and add more lime and chilli to taste, if required.
6. Ladle into bowls over a mound of rinsed, watercress.

Healthy Lunch Number 4

Energy-Revving Quinoa (Serves 2)

Ingredients

- 2-3 handfuls of cooked seasonal veg (carrots, courgettes, sweet potato etc)
- 2 lemons, halved
- Olive oil
- ½ mug quinoa
- 1 garlic clove, squashed flat and peeled
- A large handful of walnuts
- 1-2 rosemary sprigs, leaves only
- Salt & Pepper
- 1 mug water

Directions:

1. Heat a frying pan, add some olive oil and put your lemons cut side down in the pan. Get a frying pan over high heat. Brush with oil. Place your lemons in the pan, cut side down. Brown off until fragrant and browned. Set lemons aside.
2. Toast the quinoa for just a couple of minutes and add the water, season and a little oil. Simmer for 20 mins.
3. Measure 4 tbsp of olive oil into a jar or mixing bowl. Add garlic and a pinch of rosemary. Squeeze in 4 tbsp juice from the lemon. Season, shake or stir.
4. When the quinoa's done, let it steam for a couple of minutes.
5. Chop the walnuts and some rosemary leaves. Toast together in a pan until fragrant.
6. Fold your veg through the quinoa, add the lemon dressing. Fold most of the rosemary walnuts. Taste and season as required. Finish with the remaining nuts and lemon.

Healthy Lunch Number 5

Quick Baked Courgette & Feta (serves 2)

Ingredients

- A whole pack of feta
- Olive oil
- Sea salt and cracked black pepper
- A mug of couscous
- 2 courgettes
- Mint, chopped
- Flat leaf parsley, chopped
- Chives, chopped
- 1 lemon, juice only

Directions:

1. Heat your oven to 200°C/Gas 6. Put the feta in an oven proof dish, drizzle with some olive oil and season. Oven bake for 10-15 mins. Put a dry roasting tin in the oven to get it hot.
2. Boil 2 mugs of water in a pan, pour in the cous cous and cover, so it steams.
3. Use a vegetable peeler to slice ribbons of courgette. Peel until you hit the seeds in the middle, then turn. Place the ribbons in the warm roasting tin, season and add a little olive oil, place in oven for 5 mins to soften.
4. Stir the herbs and a squeeze of lemon juice to the cooked couscous. Top with the courgette ribbons and the baked feta. Sprinkle the remaining herbs over the top.

10 Healthy Dinners

Healthy Dinner Number 1

Turkey Burgers - Tomato Salad - Spinach Salad

Ingredients

- 1 pack of lean turkey mince
- 1 or 2 garlic cloves crushed
- 1 egg
- Your choice of tomatoes
- Pepper and salt to season
- 2 fresh chillies
- 1 lime
- A bunch of spring onions
- A bag of baby spinach leaves

Directions:

1. Firstly chop the chillies and herbs and mix together using your hands or a food processor with the garlic, egg and the turkey mince.
2. Season. Make the mixture into small burger shapes and leave to set in the fridge for about 1 hour. Heat some olive oil and shallow fry for about 20 minutes or until the meat is cooked through.
3. For the tomato salad, roughly chop the tomatoes into any size, add a good quality olive oil and balsamic vinegar and mix well.
4. Rinse the spinach and place in the sink in a colander, boil your kettle and then simply pour the boiling water over the spinach and shake well. Transfer to a serving bowl and drizzle with olive oil and the juice of a lime, sprinkle with rock or sea salt and mix well.

Healthy Dinner Number 2

Liver & Onions – Sweet Potato Mash – Steamed Broccoli and
Cauliflower (serves 2)

Ingredients

- Approx 150g of calves / Lamb liver
- 1 large onion
- A few sweet potatoes
- Broccoli & cauliflower

Directions

1. For the liver and onion, peel the onion and slice finely add to a
   frying pan of heated olive oil and sweat the onions by having a
   very low heat whilst cooking and season.
2. When the onions are soft, add the liver and fry for a couple of
   minutes each side. When cooked sprinkle with wine vinegar
   and let evaporate, serve nice and hot.
3. For the sweet potatoes peel and then boil until soft, drain and
   mash with a little butter and ground black pepper.
4. Steam the broccoli and cauliflower and serve.

Healthy Dinner Number 3

Cajun Style Cod/Haddock – Corn on the Cob – Sizzling Greens (serves 2)

Ingredients

- 2 cod or haddock steaks
- 1/2 lemon
- 1/2 tsp ground cumin
- 1/2 tsp mustard powder
- 1/4 tsp dried thyme
- 2 corn on the cob
- 1/2 tbsp natural yoghurt
- 2 garlic cloves crushed
- 1/2 tsp paprika
- 1/4 tsp cayenne pepper
- 1/4 tsp dried oregano
- A handful of kale
- Cabbage or large leafed spinach

Directions:

1. For the fish simply pat the steaks dry with kitchen towel, mix together the yoghurt and lime juice and brush over both sides of the fish.
2. Mix together all the herbs and spices along with 1 clove of the crushed garlic and coat both sides of the fish with the seasoning, rubbing in well.
3. Heat a non-stick frying pan with a little olive oil, add the fish and cook over a high heat for 4 minutes or until the underside is well browned. Turn over and cook for a further 4 minutes or until cooked through.
4. For the greens, shred to a size you can easily put into a wok or large frying pan. Pour a little oil into your wok or frying pan and add the other clove of crushed garlic. When it begins to sizzle add the greens and cook for a minute or two until they have started to wilt, kale will take a little longer than spinach.

Toss the greens around as they cook but be sure not to let them go brown as they will become bitter. Season and serve.

5. For the corn on the cob, boil until tender, then serve.

Healthy Dinner Number 4

Grilled Chicken with Balsamic Vinegar & Butter Griddled Chicory & Salad (serves 2)

Ingredients

- 2 chicken breast fillets
- 3 mixed peppers
- Balsamic vinegar
- A pack of chicory white or red
- 1 clove garlic
- 1/2 lemon

Directions

1. For the chicken, cover both sides of the chicken with olive oil, season with a little salt and fry for at least 2 minutes and then turn it over. Lower the heat slightly and cook for a further 8 minutes.
2. Pour over about a tablespoon of balsamic vinegar, squeeze over the lemon juice and add a couple of lumps of butter (about the size of walnuts), season and serve.
3. For the chicory, cut in half lengthways and grill or fry. Turn occasionally until charred on both sides, then remove and slice lengthways into a bowl.
4. Add salt, drizzle with olive oil and some balsamic vinegar and serve. Serve this meal with a fresh watercress or baby leaf salad.

Healthy Dinner Number 5

Grilled Lamb Chops – Sweet Carrot Mash – French Style Peas
(serves 2)

Ingredients

- Lamb chops / steaks
- 1 little gem lettuce
- 150 ml chicken stock
- Fresh thyme
- A knob of butter
- 250g carrots
- 250g frozen peas
- 1/2 lemon
- Fresh mint
- 1/2 tablespoon flour

Directions:

1. Grill the lamb until it is cooked to your liking, and remove the fat before serving.
2. For the carrot mash, simply peel and slice the carrots. In a pan add some olive oil, salt and pepper and some tips of thyme. Add the carrots and cover with boiling water and cook for about 15 minutes.
3. When the carrots are cooked, drain and mash them with a fork or masher and serve.
4. For the peas, add the butter and flour to the pan then add the chicken stock, rip up the mint leaves and add to the pan and whisk together with a whisk or fork. Slice the lettuce and add this to the pan when it has become a bubbling sauce and then add the peas and the juice of the lemon. Add a splash of boiling water, season and cover. Once the peas are cooked, serve.

\

Healthy Dinner Number 6

Crispy Salmon with Peppers – Courgette Salad – Carrots (serves 2)

Ingredients

- 1 sweet, long red pepper,
- 2 fresh red chillies
- 1 lemon
- 2 - 3 large carrots
- Fresh mint
- 1 clove of garlic
- A bunch of spring onions
- 2 fillets of salmon, skin on
- 200g Fennel seeds
- Baby courgettes
- Dried oregano

Directions

1. For the salmon, pour some olive oil into a large roasting tray. Halve and deseed the peppers.
2. Slice the pepper and the spring onions into 2cm pieces. Roughly chop the chillies.
3. Drizzle olive oil over both sides of the salmon, season and finely grate over some lemon zest. Rub these flavours all over the salmon. If necessary halve the salmon so it fits the roasting tray, then lay skin side up and arrange the slices vegetables all around it.
4. Place under a grill on the middle shelf for 14 minutes.
5. When the 14 minutes are up, remove the tray. Using a knife and your fingers carefully peel the skin away from the flesh and flip it over.
6. Add the fennel seeds, turn the peppers over then put the tray back under the grill for a further 5 minutes or until the skin is really crispy.
7. Use tongs to carefully turn the crispy salmon skin back over and cook for a further 5 minutes, then serve.

8. For the baby courgette salad, simply slice the courgettes with a speed peeler so they are lovely and thin.
9. In a bowl drizzle a good amount of olive oil, salt and pepper and the juice of 1/2 the lemon, chop up a chilli and the mint leaves then add the baby courgettes, mix together and serve.
10. For the carrot salad, peel and cut the carrots lengthways to finger size pieces and place in boiling water for a few minutes until just tender, drain and add to a serving bowl.
11. Drizzle olive oil and finely chop the clove of garlic over the carrots, add a good pinch of oregano, mix well and serve.

Healthy Dinner Number 7

Shepherds Pie with Parsnip Mash – Minty Cabbage (serves 4) This meal is great for the weekends when you have a little more time.

Ingredients

- 900g large parsnips
- 2 medium leeks
- 4 medium sized brown mushrooms
- 250ml hot vegetable stock
- 1 teaspoon ground coriander seeds
- 1 tablespoon tomato puree
- butter
- 2 tablespoons mint sauce
- 2 medium onions sliced
- 1 medium sized carrot
- 450g lean minced lamb
- A pinch of ground cumin
- 1 tablespoon garam masala
- Worcestershire sauce
- 1 savoy cabbage
- 1 bay leaf
- fresh thyme

Directions

1. For the shepherd's pie, cut the parsnips into large chunks and cook them in boiling water for about 20 minutes. Whilst they are simmering, slice and cook the onions in butter until they are soft and stir in the spices, let cook for a further couple of minutes.
2. Drain the parsnips and mash them stirring in about 50g butter and season with salt and pepper and the spiced onions.
3. Chop the leeks, peel and dice the carrots and cook in a large pan with butter until soft, this will take a little time, do not rush this part!!
4. Slice and add the mushrooms and cook for a further 5 minutes

and then add the mince to brown for about 5 minutes.

5. Add the tomato puree and a table spoon of flour, cook for a few more minutes and then add the hot vegetable stock and bring to the boil add the fresh bay leaf and thyme. Leave to simmer gently for about 25 minutes.

6. Season with salt, pepper and Worcestershire sauce, then place the mixture into a large baking dish. Cover with the parsnip mash and put in a hot oven, 190 0C / 375 0F / Gas 5 for about 25 minutes or till golden brown.

7. For the minty cabbage, simply halve the cabbage, trim and cut into 8 wedges and place in a pan. Cover with salted boiling water and cook until tender. Drain, then return to the pan with the mint sauce, some pepper and a drizzle of olive oil. Mix and serve.

Healthy Dinner Number 8

Sunday Roast – Mixed Vegetables – Roasted Sweet Potatoes (serves 4) For this meal simply use a lean joint of either lamb or beef or you can use chicken or turkey. If you are cooking for just yourself you can use a breast of chicken.

Ingredients

1 joint of meat
300g baby carrots
250g fine beans
1/2 a savoy cabbage
Butter
Sweet potatoes
1 chicken stock cube
250g runner beans
250g frozen peas
1/2 lemon

Directions

1. Roast your joint of meat according to the instructions on the meat.
2. For the roasted sweet potatoes, heat oven to 200 0C / 4000F / Gas 6. Peel and cut the sweet potato into evenly sized chunks.
3. Toss the sweet potatoes with oil in a baking dish and sprinkle over some sea or rock salt.
4. Cover and bake for half an hour, then remove cover and allow to crisp up for 10 - 20 minutes. Sprinkle over some fresh thyme leaves and serve.
5. For the mixed vegetables, simply peel and cut the carrots, put in a saucepan and cover with boiling water and add the chicken stock cube.
6. Trim the beans and cut the runner beans at an angle approx 1cm thick, cut the savoy cabbage in half and tidy up any old leaves as well as removing the stalk and then slice into thin wedges.

7. Add all of this to the pan along with peas and continue to cook.
8. When the vegetables are cooked drain and return to the pan and drizzle with olive oil, season and add a knob of butter. Finish by squeezing over lemon juice, mix well and serve.
9. To make a light gravy simply tilt the roasting pan in which you have cooked your meat and spoon out as much of the fat as possible leaving just the meat juices, place the juices into a pan and simply add either wine, dry cider or a vegetable stock cube and boil for a few moments and then pour over your dinner!

Healthy Dinner Number 9

Vegetable Curry (serves 6)

Ingredients

- 1 tablespoon olive oil
- 1 large red onion, halved and cut into thin wedges
- 2 teaspoons curry powder
- 1 teaspoon ground cumin
- 1/4 teaspoon garam masala powder
- 1/8 teaspoon cayenne pepper
- 3 cups cauliflower florets
- 1 400g can diced tomatoes with liquid
- 2 medium potatoes, peeled and cut into 1-inch cubes (about 1 ½ cups)
- 2 medium sweet potatoes, peeled and cut into 1-inch cubes (about 1 ½ cups)
- 1 ½ cups vegetable stock or water
- 1/4 teaspoon salt
- 1/4 teaspoon black pepper
- 1 cup loose-pack frozen peas
- 4 ½ cups cooked couscous or brown rice

Directions

1. Heat the olive oil in a large saucepan over medium heat. Add the onion and cook until tender, about 4 to 5 minutes. Add the curry powder, cumin, garam masala powder, and cayenne pepper. Stir well and cook for one minute.
2. Stir in the cauliflower, tomatoes, potatoes, sweet potatoes, stock, salt, and black pepper. Bring to the boil; reduce heat and simmer, covered, for 10 minutes or until the potatoes are tender. Stir in the peas; heat through. Serve over couscous or brown rice.

Healthy Dinner Number 10

Tuna Steaks with Lemon & Oregano – Chilli Greens (serves 2)

Ingredients

- 2 tuna steaks
- 1/4 teaspoon dried oregano
- 2 garlic cloves
- 4 spring onions
- Olive oil
- 1/2 tablespoon lemon juice
- A piece of ginger
- A few handfuls of greens (spinach or chard)
- 3 small red chillies

Directions

1. For the tuna, simply preheat the grill and place the grill rack about 4 inches from the heat. Brush the tuna with olive oil and season.
2. Place the tuna under the grill for about 5 minutes turning once until browned but still pink inside.
3. In a bowl, mix together a couple of tablespoons of olive oil, the lemon juice and the oregano, season to taste and pour over the tuna when it is cooked.
4. For the greens, simply heat a wok and add some olive or ground nut oil. Shred the ginger into thin pieces and add to the wok along with the sliced garlic and chopped spring onions and chillies (deseed the chillies first!).
5. Fry for about 30 seconds and then add the greens of your choice such as spinach, chard, cabbage, curly kale etc and season. Add a little water, no more than a couple of tablespoons and let it cook on a medium heat and when it is cooked through to your liking serve.

Bonus Healthy Vegetarian Dinner Number 1

Red Bean & Mushroom Burger with Fried Egg - Beetroot Salad -
Garlic Mushrooms (serves 2)

Ingredients

- 1/2 onion finely chopped
- 1/2 teaspoon cumin
- 1/4 teaspoon turmeric
- 200g can red kidney beans
- A couple of handfuls of fresh parsley
- 1/2 lemon Balsamic vinegar
- 25g butter
- 3 garlic cloves crushed
- 1/2 teaspoon dried coriander
- 500g mushrooms of your choice
- 1 tablespoon fresh chopped coriander
- 125g cooked packed beetroot
- 25g feta cheese
- Olive oil
- 2 eggs

Directions

1. For the burgers, heat some olive oil in a large frying pan and
   fry the chopped onion and crushed garlic until soft. Add the
   cumin, dried coriander and turmeric and cook for a minute
   longer stirring.
2. Add about 60g of the mushrooms chopped nice and small and
   cook until soft and dry and then remove from the heat.
3. Drain the tin of kidney beans and put them in a bowl so you
   can mash them with a fork. Add to the pan along with the fresh
   chopped coriander and season with salt and pepper. Using
   floured hands simply divide the mixture and form into burger
   shapes. Brush them with oil and grill them for about 8-10
   minutes or until cooked thoroughly.
4. Heat some olive oil in a frying pan and fry the two eggs and

lay on top of your burgers. For the garlic mushrooms, chop the remaining mushrooms into large chunks.

5. Melt the butter in a frying pan and add the 2 crushed garlic gloves. Once they start to simmer add a splash of olive oil and then the chopped mushrooms with some chopped up parsley.

6. When the mushrooms are coloured add a little more parsley and cook for a few more seconds, add a little salt and they are ready to serve.

7. For the beetroot salad, either grate the beetroot on a hand held grater or in the food processor and add to a serving bowl, drizzle with olive oil and balsamic vinegar and mix well. Crumble over the feta cheese (optional) and garnish with the remaining fresh parsley and serve.

Bonus Healthy Vegetarian Dinner Number 2

Grilled Mixed Peppers & Goats Cheese Salad - Stir Fried Chick
Peas (serves 2)

Ingredients

1 red pepper
1 yellow or orange pepper
1/2 endive (curly lettuce or similar)
175g goats cheese
400g can chickpeas
1 teaspoon paprika
200g can chopped tomatoes
1 green pepper
1/2 radicchio lettuce leaves separated
1 1/2 teaspoon white wine vinegar
2 tablespoons sunflower seeds
1 teaspoon chilli powder
1 clove garlic
225g baby spinach

Directions

1. Heat the grill and slice the peppers into pieces and grill for
   about 10 minutes. Divide the radicchio and lettuce onto your
   plates. Please note that you can use any kind of green leaves that
   you like for this salad, these lettuces work well as they are quite
   bitter in contrast with the sweet taste of the peppers.
2. In a jar mix together some olive oil and the white wine vinegar,
   add a little salt and pepper and shake well, this is your dressing.
3. Slice the goats' cheese and grill for 1 minute. Add the peppers
   and goats' cheese to your plates, dress and serve.
4. For the chick peas, simply heat a wok and add the sunflower
   seeds, dry fry until golden then remove.
5. Drain the chickpeas and then add to the wok with the chilli
   powder and paprika mix together and remove also.
6. Then add some olive oil and fry the garlic for about 30 seconds.

Add the chickpeas and stir fry for 1 minute.

7. Add the tinned tomatoes, cook for a few minutes then add the spinach. Season well and when wilted serve and scatter over the sunflower seeds.

Bonus Healthy Vegetarian Dinner Number 3

Indian Tomato & Onion Omelette with Carrots & Green Leaf Salad (serves 2)

Ingredients

- 4 Eggs
- 1 onions
- 1 tomato
- 1 tablespoon chopped coriander
- 1 lemon
- Ground Chilli
- 1 green chilli
- 3 or 4 large carrots
- 1 1/2 teaspoon cumin seeds
- Vegetable stock
- 2 bay leaves
- A bag of green leaf salad

Directions

1. For the omelette, separate the egg whites and yolks and mix the whites in a bowl to stiff peaks, then fold in the yolks.
2. Fold in a pinch of ground chilli and the green chilli and coriander finely chopped. Season with salt and ground black pepper.
3. In a frying pan heat some olive oil and when it is hot add 1/2 teaspoon of cumin seeds and fry until the start to sizzle. Add the chopped onion and cook until soft and golden.
4. Cut and add the tomato and fry for a further 2 minutes. Turn the heat to low and add the egg mixture and leave to cook the bottom side. Once the bottom is cooked place under a pre heated grill to cook the rest of the way through and serve.
5. For the carrots with cumin and lemon, simply peel and cut into cork size pieces and put them in a saucepan. Add enough vegetable stock to the pan to come half way up the carrots and then add1 teaspoon of cumin seeds, the zest and juice of the

lemon plus the bay leaves. Season with a little salt and let them boil and cover for 10-15 minutes

6. Serve with a fresh green leaf salad of your choice, drizzled with olive oil and lemon.

Dan Aguilera

Chapter Seven

Stop Talking About It and Start Doing It

My pet hate, apart from someone failing to replace a toilet roll, is people failing to do what they start out to do. Personally, I think it shows the strength of a person (or lack of it), especially when they give up very shortly after starting. However, I am not saying that you should continue to run a marathon with an injury, but simply that when committing to change you have to follow it through.

How complicated is it to eat right?

....

....

The answer is that it's only as complicated as you choose to make it.

The biggest reason why people don't change their diet is that they have to take responsibility for their actions – and this is something that scares them.

There are endless 'reasons' why we give up in certain

situations …

Self-reflection has obviously played an important part of your journey thus far, hence the reason why you are reading this right now. So, thinking that things are too hard or denying yourself the opportunity to succeed by thinking, "This will never work for me," is natural, but the thoughts in your head directly influence the actions you take and therefore the outcomes you experience in reality. If you think it's too hard, it is; if you think it won't work for you, it won't. With this in mind, it's the steps you take to overcome this negative mind-set that makes the difference between making changes for the better or staying where you are.

"Whatever the mind of man can conceive and believe, it can achieve." – Napoleon Hill

Think about it for a moment; when you're in the gym, have you ever noticed that some people get on the treadmill every day and continue to do the same thing day in and day out for no apparent gain? They keep going but very little change appears to be happening, so why is this? Well, the bottom line is that they're failing to take the steps needed to generate positive change. They run, and then they eat poorly, so they then run again, and then they eat poorly again … and so it goes on, but nothing actually changes. They're stuck in that vicious cycle and getting nowhere. Continuing to do the same things will continue to bring you the same results – are the things you're doing now bringing you the results you want?

" The definition of insanity is doing the same thing over and over again and expecting a different result"

Also, I know I've mentioned this previously but think about food packaging and labelling; anything that can be considered a remotely 'healthy' option will be proudly advertised on the packaging. But here's the thing – anything that's a truly healthy option won't come with a wrapper that tells you so. We all know that something that sounds too good to be true probably isn't true (e.g. this packet contains delicious sticky toffee pudding and only three calories) but yet we tend to believe what we're told when we read information on packaged foods produced by well-known and respected food manufacturers.

To break away from this pattern of believing what you read, remember that food manufacturers are business people and they're in the business of making money just like any other business. A good business is one that sustains employment and has the ability to grow and increase profit margins – the food manufacturing business is no different. It's for this reason that the only way to be sure of what you're eating is to prepare your own foods from scratch, preferably from their raw state. The more processes a food product has been through, the less nutritional value it will contain – simple.

Let's face it, we can all come up with any number of reasons why we'll never achieve whatever it is we want, and we can spend days, hours and even years looking back at where things went wrong or where things all just seemed a little bit too hard, but trust me, if you commit to changing your diet today, it's never too late to achieve the life you want. Choose to eat the foods that represent the colourful, vibrant life you want to live.

The colours of your food represent the type of life you will live – dark, dull, flat, and toxic, or bright, shapely, and packed full of energy.

Okay, we've established that you really are a by-product of the foods you eat so now it's time to focus on the amount of food you should be eating. Once again, this is really nothing more than common sense, but we know that common sense doesn't always prevail. Remember, eating right is only as complicated as you choose to make it. Eating the right amount of food doesn't need to be complicated – if it looks a lot then it probably is, and that's it. If the food on your plate is piled high and/or spilling over the edges, then the likelihood is you're over consuming. If you can see empty space around the edge of your plate and your food is relatively flat, rather than piled high in the centre, then you can be fairly sure you're on the right track.

When it comes to making good food choices, I like to use the phrase, "If a rabbit can eat it, then so can I" but another phrase I keep in the back of my mind is, "You never see a skinny rabbit." The relevance of this is that the amount of food you eat is just as important as the types of food you eat, in terms of eating a healthy diet. Just because a food is fresh, vibrant and healthy does not mean that you can eat as much of it as you want, and it's a fact that you can still become obese on a vegan/vegetarian diet.

It must also be remembered that the same principle applies to drinks in your diet. Only water and natural juices should be consumed and fizzy, chemical-rich pops should be avoided.

Personally, my liquid consumption now consists only of homemade juices or smoothies, coffee, and unlimited amounts of water.

Fact: if you OVER EAT you GET FAT

Let's talk a little more about movement. Again, this is really basic stuff and makes absolute sense, but the more you move the more energy you burn. This is not rocket science, but, the more energy you burn the less energy (in the form of fat) your body will store away for a rainy day. If you fail to move then you fail to use energy and the end result is unwanted weight gain. The worst thing about weight gain is that it's like a snowball – the more your body stores fat the more fat it piles on. Why? Well, your body has no other use for it because it already has plenty of stored energy (fat) in reserve. In a recent study, those who failed to exercise on a regular basis cited a lack of time as a major restriction. However, the same study revealed that the amount of time currently spent watching television and browsing social media websites was double that of time dedicated to exercise. This highlights the fact that committing to getting more exercise is not a question of having to find more time, it's a question of making better use of the time you have.

Hard fact: the less you move, the bigger you WILL get!

Use food to support you, not kill you ... this is a concept that can create a significant emotional struggle. I know this from personal experience and I know full well that when you're feeling a little low or things are not quite turning out the way you want, the first stop is often junk food.

To my mind, the reason for this is very simple. Just as a drug offers a temporary activation of chemicals and a firing of certain things within the mind, the same happens with the chemicals found in typical junk foods. In 2013, a Liverpool University study identified a number of harmful chemicals that directly affect the central nervous system. The very same chemicals were found in a number of popular children's sweets. They include: (E133); (E104); (E110); (E124), and (E122) to name just a few.

These chemicals are drugs and while they don't affect the body in the same way as Class A drugs, they do have an effect on the natural chemical balance within the body and they do cause a high. So why do we reach for the sweets or junk food when feeling low? It's not because we need them, but because our past neurological memories have made us aware of the highs we will experience as a result of eating them. Through common sense we know that eating something artificial is never going to provide any meaningful health benefit, and we also know that we're still going to feel low after eating it. The bottom line is that if you're feeling unhappy, bored, depressed or just under the weather in general, no amount of junk food can actually change the way you feel.

Hard fact: those who consume a poor diet are more likely to suffer from long-term negative emotional conditions.

Of course, the problem is that many of us fall into the trap of believing that it's 'comfort food' that makes us feel better. So how do we break out of this trap? In the world of NLP (Neuro-Linguistic Programming) we use something called a pattern interrupt. Basically, this means you replace the usual habit of consuming junk with a new habit of consuming something that's genuinely good for you instead. I know this sounds incredibly simple, but eating right does not need to be complicated. Just do it and experience the positive results for yourself. There's no 'magic' or miracle cure, but a simple change of habit can bring about miraculous changes for the better in the way you feel. The better you feel, the more likely it is you'll continue to make the right food choices without even consciously thinking about it.

Start looking in the right place ... something that never ceases to amaze me is the way that many high street shops effectively hide genuinely healthy foods. Just the other day, I was looking for the vegan/vegetarian section in a popular shop and I eventually found it in-between the pharmacy and the pre-cooked meat deli. Now, not only does this not make any sense, it confirms my belief that larger corporations don't actually want to promote genuinely healthy eating. You see, they don't want to promote natural super-foods when there's far more money to be made from promoting packaged (highly processed) foods that proudly proclaim they're the 'healthy option' on the label. This isn't a witch-hunt; you can make up your own mind when you next go out shopping. Just try looking for the genuinely healthy foods on the shelves and see how much longer it takes you.

Another thing to explore as you do your food shopping is the actual origin of the produce on display. We've already discussed the benefits of shopping local, but as you begin to pay more attention to the foods available in supermarkets, you'll begin to find ways to source foods that have spent the least amount of time in transit or storage. If you have children, the supermarket can be as good a place as any to begin building their understanding of the true meaning of healthy eating.

Interesting note: a 2013 British Nutritional Foundation study revealed that almost one third of primary school pupils in the UK think that cheese is made from plants, and one quarter think that fish fingers come from chicken or pigs. The study also revealed that nearly one in 10 secondary school pupils think that tomatoes grow underground, and that there's confusion over the source of many diet staples such as pasta and bread with many younger pupils stating they believed them to be made from meat.

Re-education, re-education, re-education ... commit to exploring and accepting anything that will make you a better person. It doesn't have to be 'trendy' and it doesn't have to be right for the guy next door, it only has to be right for you. Any change you make that brings even just one tiny positive aspect with it is a change that's worth it.

The 4 Seasons of Weight Loss

"A setback ain't nothing but a setup for a comeback"
Dan Aguilera

This is something that I talk to my members about all of the time.

You have to think of your weight loss journey like the 4 weather seasons, sometimes it summer, winter, autumn and spring.

How does this relate to weight loss, you are not going to lose weight all of the time, sometimes you will stay the same (Spring), sometimes you will go up and down (Autumn) sometimes you will gain weight (Winter) and sometimes you will lose weight (Summer).

To appreciate the summer you have got to go trough winter, so focus your energy on just doing the right things often enough and the results will come.

Dan Aguilera

Mindful Change

Over the next few days, I want you to work through the following exercises and immerse yourself into the patterns of changing your thinking. These exercises have been designed to help you change to new and supportive patterns.

You can do one per day, one every other day or even spread them out over the coming weeks – it doesn't matter. All that's important is that you accept you are accountable for your actions and that the commitment you make right now will generate your change in the future.

Mindful Change Exercise Number 1

Task: Answer the following:

Why is weight loss important to me?

....

....

....

....

....

....

. . . .

Having covered this in detail, we know that change will become easier after a period of time. To help keep you on track, I'd like you to write down the following rules. These should be placed prominently in the locations you are most likely to frequent on a daily basis.

Action 1 – I should only eat when I'm in a happy state of mind. If I'm not happy then I should change my state before consuming food. If in doubt, drown it out (drink a glass of water with ice).

Action 2 – I will chew my food consciously, this will ensure that the messages reach my stomach and allow time for the mind to let me know I'm full.

Action 3 – I will give myself plenty of time to eat and prepare food; if I don't have the time then I will remove social media and TV from my life until I have the time.

Action 4 – I will always make myself consciously aware of what I am eating. Unless I know exactly what is in it, I won't be eating it. Who knows, it could be poison!

Action 5 – I will keep an honest and up to date diary of the food I am consuming, this includes everything that passes my lips – good, bad and neutral.

Although they seem overly simplistic and you may feel little need to write them down, the constant conscious reminder helps to improve your awareness of what you are doing and acts to change negative habits through re-patterning normal behaviours.

Mindful Change Exercise Number 2

Task: Answer the following:

What do I want my body to look like and why?

....

....

....

....

....

....

....

We have already established that weight loss (Fat Loss) should not be the primary goal but rather the achievement of a healthy and supportive body.

Action 1 – Everything I eat is seen as energy and should be supportive to my mind and body: what can I do today to ensure that I only choose quality foods?

Action 2 – What can I do today to ensure that my body receives the right amount of movement required to tone and increase my cardiovascular performance?

Action 3 – What changes can I make today to the way I look to improve my own self-confidence?

Action 4 – Why do I deserve to be happy, loved and fulfilled in my life?

It's a fact that the more you work on you, the better you will be. Avoid the temptation to see yourself as a finished project; you have a number of years left to continue improving and live a better and more fulfilling life than you have already.

"Success is a Journey, not a Destination"

Mindful Change Exercise Number 3

Task: Answer the following:

What conscious adjustments to food should I be making?

....

....

....

....

....

....

....

We know what we *should* be eating yet time and time again we kid ourselves that what we are actually eating won't matter – WRONG. Everything you consume – from a leftover chicken-dipper off your child's plate to a bottle of coke gulped down for a quick energy fix – matters.

Action 1 – Today I will be making a conscious choice to eat only 'real' foods rather than processed or 'fake' foods.

Action 2 – What can I remove from my usual working day that will remove all temptation to snack or consume food that has no positive nutritional value?

Action 3 – What new beliefs can I have about my body; why is now the right time to make the changes needed to improve my life for the better?

Action 4 – What can I do to reduce stress within my life today and begin moving forward with my life?

Conscious awareness of the foods we consume is essential to ensure that we continually make adjustments. Just as a ship requires adjustments to the sail, we also require the same level of conscious commitment to staying on course.

Mindful Change Exercise Number 4

Task: Answer the following:

What can I do to ensure that I am eating the right amount of food?

....

....

....

....

....

....

....

Eating the right amount of food is essential in terms of overall health. Consuming too much will lead to your body storing the excess as fat but eating too little will slow your metabolism.

Action 1 – What should I be eating per day to support my metabolism and the gradual reduction of body fat?

Action 2 – What can I do today to ensure that I'm not consuming food at the wrong time of the day?

Action 3 – How does planning help me with the right food choices?

Action 4 – How am I able to manage the intake of healthy food when eating out or without food that I have prepared?

Action 5 – Why am I eating healthy and nutritionally rich food?

Thinking in terms of 'actions' alters the way we communicate with ourselves, and by asking better questions we achieve better answers and better outcomes as a result.

Mindful Change Exercise Number 5

Task: Answer the following:

Why am I so committed to change right now?

....

....

....

....

....

What am I going to do to ensure that I never relapse?

....

....

....

....

....

How will I respond to people who look at my actions in a negative light?

....

....

....

. . . .

. . . .

. . . .

. . . .

. . . .

Avoid the temptation to do more than you can, it will very rarely attract the results you want. This programme is not like other programmes, you are not restricted by time or goals, so take a moment to pause and think about what is realistically possible. If you have invested 20 years into achieving the weight you are now, accept that it's unrealistic to expect to lose unwanted weight in just a couple of weeks. Commit to getting on board for the journey and choose to make every change a lasting change.

The time is now and now is the time to begin discovering the best you it's possible to be.

But a word of warning: there are no quick fix solutions that support a long-term weight loss or lifestyle solution and there is no magic pill you can take over 12 weeks that will reverse the effects of poor lifestyle choices. Lasting change takes time; time to change your habits and time to adjust to new ways of being.

The best time to plant a tree was 20 years ago. The second best time is now. – Chinese Proverb

Annex A.

Exercises

Lunges:

1. Stand with your feet shoulder width apart and your hands on your hips.
2. Step forward with one leg, flexing (bending) the knees to drop your hips. Descend until your rear knee almost touches the ground. Your posture should remain upright, and your front knee should stay above the front foot.
3. Drive through the heel of your lead foot and extend (straighten) both knees to raise yourself back up.
4. Push up and go back to the starting position, repeating the lunge on the opposite leg.

Squat:

1. Stand with your feet shoulder width apart. This will be your starting position.
2. Begin the movement by flexing your knees and hips, sitting back with your hips as if about to sit down in an imaginary chair.
3. Continue down to full depth if you are able, and then quickly reverse the motion to return to the starting position. As you squat, keep your head and chest up.

Squat Jump:

1. Stand with your feet shoulder width apart, and squat down

keeping your torso upright and your head up. This will be your starting position.

2. From the bottom jump in the air, but avoid jumping unnecessarily high. As your feet contact the ground, absorb the impact through your legs and back into the squat, and jump again.

Plank:

1. Get into a prone position (face down) on the floor, supporting your weight on your toes and your forearms. Your arms are bent with the elbows directly below the shoulders.
2. Keep your body straight – and hold. Make sure you pull your stomach muscles in tight. Maintain this position for as long as possible. To decrease difficulty, place your knees on the ground.

Press Up:

1. Position yourself on your hands and knees on the floor. Adopt a press up (push up) position with your arms shoulder and a half width apart, bend your arms lowering your chest towards the ground, feel the stretch across your chest then push up to the start position. Make sure you keep your body (back) straight.

Bent Over Row:

1. Holding a pair of dumbbells. Bend your knees slightly and bend over from the waist and push your bum out behind you keeping your back straight.
2. Pull the dumbbells towards you either side of your chest. Retract the shoulder blades and squeeze them together.
3. Lower the dumbbells and repeat the exercise.

Shoulder Press:

1. Stand with your feet shoulder width apart; hold a pair of dumbbells on your shoulders with your palm facing forward. Pull your abs in nice and tight.
2. Press the dumbbells directly overhead by extending through the

elbow, and meet the dumbbells at the top to gain full range of motion

3. Lower the pressed dumbbells to the starting position and immediately press them to the top again.

Upright Row:

1. Holding a pair of dumbbells, stand up straight holding the dumbbells in front of you with your palms facing your thighs, this will be your starting position.
2. Raise the dumbbells up towards your chin with elbows leading the movement keeping your knuckles facing down. Aim to raise the dumbbells to a height that's in line with your chin, and your elbows above your shoulders, exhale as you lift. Tip: as you lift the dumbbells, your elbows should always be higher than your forearms. Keep your torso still (no rocking or swinging to assist the lift) and pause for a second at the top of the movement.
3. Lower the dumbbells slowly back down to the starting position. Inhale as you do so.
4. Repeat for the recommended amount of repetitions.

Bicep Curl:

1. Stand up straight with a dumbbell in each hand at arm's length – arms by your sides. Keeping your elbows close to your torso, rotate the palms of your hands until they are facing forward. This will be Keeping the upper arms fixed in place, curl the weights while contracting your biceps to raise your hands towards your shoulders. Exhale as you do so. Continue to raise the weights until your biceps are fully contracted and the dumbbells are at shoulder level. Hold the contracted position for a brief pause as you squeeze your biceps.
2. Slowly begin to lower the dumbbells back to the starting position, inhale as you go.
3. Repeat for the recommended amount of repetitions.

Triceps Extensions:

1. Holding a dumbbell with both hands, stand with your feet

shoulder width apart, pull your abs in tight.

2. Bring the dumbbell up to shoulder height and then extend the arm so that the weight is being held over your head with a straight arm.

3. Bend your elbow slightly so that the little finger is facing the ceiling. This will be your starting position.

4. Slowly lower the dumbbell behind your head by bending your elbow, keeping your elbows close to your head. Inhale as you perform this movement and pause when your triceps are fully stretched.

5. Return to the starting position by flexing your triceps, exhale as you raise the dumbbell. Tip: it is imperative that only the forearm moves. The upper arm should remain in position next to your head at all times.

6. Repeat for the recommended amount of repetitions.

Crawl Out:

1. Standing with your feet shoulder width apart, bend your knees; place your hands on the floor.

2. Crawl out five paces then crawl back in.

3. Stand up back to the start position, then repeat.

Burpees

1. Stand with your feet hip width apart and your arms down by your side.

2. Lower into a squat position and place your hands flat on the floor in front of you.

3. Kick your legs out backwards into a press up position and lower your chest to the floor.

4. Push your chest back up to the press up position as you jump both feet forward to return to the squat position.

5. Jump up and raise both hands over your head.

Crunches:

1. Lay flat on your back with your toes on the ground; lift your heels up with your knees bent at a 90-degree angle.

2. Place your hands lightly on either side of your head keeping your elbows in. Tip: don't lock your fingers behind your head as this will lead to pulling on your neck.
3. While pushing the small (lower) of your back down into the floor to better isolate your abdominal muscles, begin to roll your shoulders off the floor.
4. Continue to push down as hard as you can with your lower back as you contract your abdominals and exhale. Your shoulders should come up off the floor only about four inches, and your lower back should remain on the floor. At the top of the movement, contract your abdominals tightly and keep the contraction for a second. Tip: focus on slow, controlled movement – don't cheat yourself by using momentum.
5. After the one second contraction, slowly return to the starting position as you inhale.
6. Repeat for the recommended amount of repetitions.

Oblique Crunch:

1. Lay flat on your back with your toes on the ground; lift your heels up with your knees bent at a 90-degree angle. Straighten one leg out in front of you and keep it 6 inches off the ground
2. Place your hands lightly on either side of your head keeping your elbows in. Tip: don't lock your fingers behind your head as this will lead to pulling on your neck.
3. While pushing the small (lower) of your back down into the floor to better isolate your abdominal muscles, begin to roll your shoulders off the floor.
4. Continue to push down as hard as you can with your lower back as you contract your abdominals and exhale. Your shoulders should come up off the floor only about four inches, and your lower back should remain on the floor. At the top of the movement, contract your abdominals tightly and keep the contraction for a second. Tip: focus on slow, controlled movement – don't cheat yourself by using momentum.
5. After the one second contraction, slowly return to the starting position as you inhale.
6. Repeat for the recommended amount of repetitions and then change legs.

Reverse Curl:

1. Lay flat on your back, lift your feet off the ground, keeping your knees together
2. Place your hands on the floor, raise your knees towards your chest
3. Rolling up so the your bum lifts off the ground, roll back down in a controlled movement to the start position and then repeat.

Cross Over Crunch:

1. Lay flat on your back with your legs straight; place your hands at the base of your back.
2. Lift your feet off the ground, open your legs as wide as you can, then bring them back in crossing your feet over and repeat.

Bicycle Crunches:

1. Lay flat on your back with your legs straight; place your hands at the base of your back.
2. Lift your feet off the ground; Begin a cycle motion by bringing your left knee inwards your chest while simultaneously straightening out your right leg away from your body.
3. Return to the start position then continue the cycle motion by this time bringing your right knee inwards to meet your chest while straightening out your left leg at the same time.
4. Continue alternating in this manner until all of the recommended repetitions for each side have been completed.

Kick Outs:

1. Kneel on the floor or on an exercise mat and bend at the waist with your arms extended in front of you, in order to get into a kneeling push-up position, but with your arms spaced at shoulder width. Your head should be looking forward and the bend of the knees should create a 90-degree angle between the hamstrings and the calves. This will be your starting position.
2. As you exhale, lift up your right leg until the hamstrings are in

line with your back while maintaining the 90-degree angle in your knee. Contract the glutes (bum) throughout this movement and hold the contraction at the top and extend your leg to the side, kicking out

3. Return to the starting position as you inhale and then repeat with the left leg.
4. Continue to alternate legs until all of the recommended repetitions have been performed.

Hip Raises:

1. Lay flat on your back with your feet flat on the ground; with your knees bent at a 90-degree angle.
2. Lift your hips up towards the ceiling, and tense your bum at the top of the motion, hold at the top for 3 seconds before lowering back to the start position,
3. Continue until recommended repetitions have been performed.

About Dan

Dan Aguilera is a respected health and weight loss expert who has been transforming bodies and changing lives with incredible success for over a decade. In 2014 his clients lost a total of 1278 stone – the equivalent of two African male elephants.

He believes that everyone can have the body they want by following Four simple principles.

- Progressive Nutrition
- Progressive Exercise
- Education & Support
- Lifestyle & Behaviour Change

The Ultimate Weight Loss Solution removes myths and common misconceptions, and highlights simple to follow 'high-street' diet advice, with a system that is practical, proven, fun and great for lasting weight loss.

http://www.ultimateu-fitness.co.uk
www.facebook.com/UltimateUFitness

Printed in Great Britain
by Amazon.co.uk, Ltd.,
Marston Gate.